Get more resources at:

www.LloydHBell.com

Dedication

This book is dedicated with love to my

mother Joyce M. Bell, my aunt Rachel

Ngali-Marsala and to the parents of those

who are struggling with addiction and

Substance Use Disorders of their children.

PREFACE

This book is written by a son who was once caught in the grips of addiction now in recovery over 13 years as he writes. I write this book to parents because my heart goes out to those dealing with an addicted child. It is my desire to give insight, understanding, and hope for you parents who may pick up this book. It is my goal to articulate to you certain things in a way that your child may not be in place to. Many parents find themselves at a loss, frustrated, and heartbroken as they watch addiction destroy the lives of their children and cause pain to those around them. This book is an effort to shed light on some of the questions parents may have.

At the time as I write this book, I am 38 years of age, and I have lived what many are experiencing now with their children. As I look back at the pain, I caused my mother and father during my active addiction it hurts to recall those dark days. I know my parents often wondered if I would ever "get my act together" or straighten up and fly right. They often would look at me baffled as to how I could continue down the self-destructive road I was on. I am sure like other parents they wondered if I could see the mess I was making of my life and the lives I was impacting in a negative way. Could I not see what drugs and alcohol had done to my relatives and how hard it was on the family? Did I not have a loving and supporting family? Was I not raised better than this? If so, then what was my problem and how could they help?

I truly believe if you picked up this book you are like many loving and desperate parents who would recover for their children if they could. You would give your left arm if you thought it would get your child off the "stuff". But you are probably at the point or close to the edge of hopelessness which is compounded by the confusion of how it came to this. So while I do not claim to be an expert on all things addiction, please allow me to share with you some things that may shed light and offer some hope in your current situation. I do not desire to be the poster child for recovery or branded a hero for the cause. My sole purpose for writing is because YOU the PARENTS have been laid on my heart. And I only have three prayers: 1) that the story of my struggle will help to ease yours. 2) That your child will get well and recover, and 3) that you **never lose hope.**

The Serenity Prayer

God, grant me the serenity to

accept the things I cannot change,

Courage to change the things I can,

and the wisdom to know the difference.

You may ask why I started off this book with the serenity prayer. This prayer can be found in many forms and has been used throughout the years by addiction support groups like Alcoholics Anonymous and family support groups such as Ala Non. This is for many good reasons. One reason this prayer is so utilized is because acceptance, courage, and wisdom are all attributes that will be needed when dealing with addiction or an addicted loved one. Another reason I chose this way to begin the book is because I am a big believer in the old saying, "Prayer Changes Things".

I come from a praying family. This does not mean we were exempt from the trials of life or the horrors of addiction. In fact, addiction and mental illness have plagued my family for generations. Now I know if any of my kin folk are reading this they may be thinking TMI. However, it all ties into my story and what needs to said. Now, my mother and grandmother are what I call prayer warriors of the highest degree. I know for a fact I would not be writing a jot or tittle without their prayers for me when I was in my active addiction. I was hell-bent on my own demise and destruction while they were steadfast in praying for my protection and deliverance from the bondage of addiction.

What does this have to do with the serenity prayer or my child you may be asking? If you have an addicted child, it may have been some time since you have experienced peace or serenity. It is more likely than not that you have been caught up in the drama, fall out, and repercussions associated with having a child in active addiction. Are you lying awake at night worrying if you will get some type of bad news concerning your child? Do you worry about the well-being of your grandchildren? Are you constantly asking "who is looking after my grand babies?" What about the concerns you have for your addicted child's legal situation? Why does it seem you are more concerned about them going to jail than they are? How many times have you said I will not bail you out of trouble again only to run to the rescue? Parents, are you starting to get the picture? What does this constant state of worry, anxiety, and fear do to you? Has it affected your health and drained you? When is the last time you knew serenity?

Getting caught in the whirlwind of an addicted child robs parents of their peace of mind, trust, and can negatively affect their health. When people most often employ prayer is when they have done all they can do. In support groups, one of the first things they do at meetings is, to begin with prayer and end with prayer. For some, it may just be words being recited. But for some, it is a reminder that the peace that surpasses all understanding comes from God and that the type of acceptance, courage and wisdom needed in this fight is also His to bestow.

Something Parents Need to Know

Here are some things your addicted child cannot tell you right now as it relates to the Serenity Prayer. If you are not a praying person, I would suggest you become one and let the serenity prayer be one of the first prayers you learn. If you get nothing from this book but the serenity prayer you have gained more than you know. This simple prayer has the ability to shift your thinking, increase your ability to cope, and provide you an understanding that ushers in peace in the midst of the storm.

The serenity to accept the things you cannot change. This is the first of many paradigm shifts that need to take place for parents if you are to come out of this ordeal in your right mind. There were many things you were able to protect us from when we were younger. You were able as parents to many times keep us out of harm's way and ensure that things worked in our favor. Today you are hard-pressed and fighting to hold on to the idea there is something you can say or do to help your child get back on track and get well. It is understandable that you as a parent would try all within your power to change your child's situation. However, when coming against addiction, your love for your child, pleadings, and all the power you can muster is not enough. This may be a hard reality to accept. In fact, that's why it is the first part of the serenity prayer.

Coming to the grips that in your own strength and all that you have to offer won't stop your addicted child from continuing down the destructive road is a hard pill to swallow. It goes against every fiber in your being as a parent. It creates an inner turmoil like no other. Do I let my child go to the wayside and possibly die or do I die trying to change their predicament? Some parents have picked up this book hoping to find out "what can I do"? Well, the very first thing you can do is to accept the insanity of addiction can infiltrate the lives of those who are not addicted. This happens as parents continue to do the same things over and over and expect different results.

You will know that you have been sucked into the insanity of the addiction if you are continually trying to bail your child out of situations they have gotten themselves in due to their addiction time after time. Regardless of how many times their track record has shown that they will go right back to the same behavior that got them in that situation, you do the same thing. Your addicted child will never say to you, "Hey mom and dad what you are doing is not helping so try something else". If they are in active addiction, they will continue to capitalize on the fact that you as a parent have not come to grips that you cannot change them in your own power. Your child will never come out and say, "I am in the grips of an illness that has me self-centered and set on destruction and I will use you up if you let me". However the sooner a parent accepts this they can begin to change the things they can.

The courage to change the things I can comes into play as parents start to accept the things they have no power to change. Here we start get into the question, "What can I do as a parent?" One of the first things a parent can do is to <u>do something different for a change</u>. One of the biggest and most courageous things a parent can do is to stop rescuing their addicted child from rock bottom. Rescuing your child from their rock bottom means you continually step in so that situations don't get as bad as you fear they could. It's as if you are still trying to keep us from playing with fire like you did when were younger. Instead, parents often keep the addicted child from consequences that may be that very jarring experience that causes us enough pain to seek help.

Here are some practical things you can change as a parent. You can <u>change your stance</u> on what you will allow in your home. One day my father, "flipped the script" on me. Being a recovering addict himself and a minister he got to the point where he could no longer take my disregard to his home and his sobriety and kicked me out of his home. Now, my mother held her peace, but she was not very happy because she wanted me nearby. However, my father had the courage to change his stance and employ "tough love" as some call it. Up to that point, my father's stance was one that allowed me to jeopardize his sobriety and serenity in the name of love and in efforts to keep me from harm's way. In my case, that led me to spiral down to my rock bottom sooner which I will discuss more a little later.

Another thing that a parent can change is their tone. There is a time for tender tones, and there is a time for a firm and urgent tone. If there is no firmness and urgency in your manner of expressing the severity of how your child's addiction is impacting you, they will often continue to minimize and even deny the need for a change. Please understand that I speak from experience. I can recall after my father kicked me out I stayed with friends until I landed at one of my favorite aunt's house. My cousins and I were grown, and we drank and partied like it was nobody's business. The only problem was I was the only one who didn't know when to stop. When everyone else sobered up and went to work, I laid around waiting until they would get off to party at night. I would go to stores and steal alcohol to get me through the day if I couldn't bum any money or find someone willing to smoke their weed with me.

One day I found myself in jail again, for what I honestly don't recall. But my aunt and uncle came and bailed me out. Before I could get sentimental my uncle (RIP) looked me square in the eyes and said you need to get your #$%^& together. Mind you this was one of the coolest uncles I knew. He would drink a brew with us and kick it occasionally with us "boys in the hood". So when he changed his tone, it struck a chord in me. I said if Uncle Bootsie says I need help it must be serious because he was as nonjudgmental and laid back as they come and never made me feel unwelcomed. That all changed when he changed his tone with me.

In efforts, not to digress I will share a handful more of small things that a parent can change if they have the courage to do so. You may think it strange, but you can change your locks. Yes, the locks on your house. There are parents who know exactly why I mention this. You can change the place you keep your valuables. You can change your yes to a no. Sometimes the hardest thing to tell your addicted child is no. The last thing I will touch on is extremely hard to change but it will help parents greatly if they put it into practice. You can change your "buttons". By buttons, I mean your "hot buttons" or "*empathy buttons*". When we are in active addiction, an addicted child knows which buttons to push. This is how the addicted child manipulates the parent. Try changing those buttons or identifying and dealing with those sensitive areas that are used to manipulate you as parents. The next time the addicted child tries to get a rise out of you by pushing that button, it won't be there, and you won't have to feel horrible for falling for it again. One example is the utilization of shame and guilt. Or maybe it is bringing up your past. These tactics are what we use to confuse the truth and a smoke screen to mask that we will say or do anything for the next one.

This is where **the wisdom to know the difference** from the serenity prayer comes in. This type of wisdom knows as a parent that you cannot change the fact that you love your addicted child, but you can change how you show that love. It is the wisdom that opens your eyes to when addiction has twisted your efforts to love into detrimental forms of enabling. There is a difference between loving someone to death and *loving someone to death*. Addiction has already infiltrated the life of your child and taken them hostage, and if you are not careful, it will seem as if you have no recourse but to become a slave to the whims of your child's addiction in the name of love. This type of wisdom is in opposition to the saying, "don't just stand there, do something". It is the type of wisdom that will keep you from repeating the same thing and expecting different results. You will understand that having unrealistic expectations set you up for heartache and resentments. You begin to acknowledge that you cannot change your addicted child, but you can change how to react to and deal with them.

It has been said that King Solomon's prayer request was to be granted wisdom and God granted him great wisdom. In fact 1 Kings 4:30 states that "Solomon's wisdom was greater than the wisdom of all the people of the East and greater than all the wisdom of Egypt." One of the most powerful things Solomon wrote that pertains to your situation as parents of addicted children is not in found in his Proverbs. It is found in the following passages of Ecclesiastes when Solomon writes, "There is a time to a time to scatter stones and a time to gather them, a time to hug and a time to stop hugging. A time to start looking and a time to stop looking, a time to keep and a time to throw away. A time to tear apart and a time to sew together, a time to keep quiet and a time to speak out."

King Solomon is an example of how praying for wisdom can lead to the understanding that there is a need to *"know the difference"*. When my mother began to understand that she could not change me and my father realized that what he was doing was not going to change me they changed their approach. They still loved me unconditionally, but they did something different for a change. Instead of killing themselves trying to change a person who was not ready for change they turned me over to the care of the loving God of their understanding. It may have seemed to others that they turned me over to the brutal illness of addiction but in reality, they were trusting in the power of God to do for me what they could not.

Knowing the difference means you know deep down that your decision while painful is what is needed for your child and your sanity. Others may not be able to differentiate between leaving your loved one to their own devices verses surrendering and trusting a Power greater than yourself. A child in active addiction will most certainly be at the top of the list of people who will not agree with any choice that interrupts feeding their addiction. In this state we will paint you a horrific picture of what will happen to us if you don't enable our continued use. We will try to make you feel as if it will be your fault that we have to do dangerous and degrading things to get our fix. But the wisdom to know the difference will not allow a parent to be shamed, blamed, or gamed.

What my parents did took unconventional, and some might say supernatural acceptance, courage, and wisdom on their part. There was a peace that they experienced when they made this shift. This serenity is what the Serenity Prayer is all about. This is not to say that all fears and concerns will disappear without a trace forever. You will still yearn for your loved one to change and get better and even shed tears for them at times. But the Serenity Prayer will help you cope and navigate while dealing with your child with a peace that is hard to explain and understand.

A Time to Hate

"There is a time to love and a time to hate" –King

Solomon

We have already established that you would not be reading this book if you did not love and want the best for your addicted child. So this section of the book is not aimed to change that or discourage loving your child. Instead, it is to shed the light and expose an ugly side of addiction in a manner that you may not be accustomed to. What I write in this section may change the way you see things as it relates to the child caught in the grips of active addiction. This is not something your child is currently at liberty to disclose.

First of all, you may have heard the saying that addiction is a cunning, baffling and powerful illness. But what does this truly mean? What is the so-called insidious nature of addiction that people are talking about? The word insidious expresses the fact that addiction has the capability to deceive and entrap people unawares. I allude to this in the section above. Remember how I talk about the way addiction seems to inconspicuously creep into the lives of those who are non-addicts? This is why you will often hear people say addiction is a family disease. Because addiction has the capability to not only take over the life of the child but also the lives of the parent of the one in active addiction.

Here is a hard, ugly truth about addiction. If your child is in full blown active addiction, **you are no longer dealing with your child, but you are dealing the addiction**. Let me repeat that when the addiction has taken over, you are not dealing with your child anymore. This is another crucial point that parents need to take away from this book if nothing else. It is something your child may not be able to articulate at this time because the addiction has them in such bondage. If your child was able to speak truly about the nature of addiction, they would warn you. They would tell you that until they get help they are subject to lie, steal from you and hurt you in more ways than one to get the next fix. They would tell you to keep your distance until they are in a place to accept your help because if not they will make you a victim of their addiction.

Instead, addiction in its truest form left unchecked manifests by causing your child to be so self-centered that they could care less about what happens to you as long as they get their next fix. In this state we could care less if our actions cause our parents pain, incarceration, or homelessness when the urges hit. Parents you need to realize at this stage of addiction you are no longer dealing with your "baby boy" or" baby girl". You are now dealing with a hideous beast that has surfaced due the addiction that resembles your child. It sounds more like a science fiction to some at this point I know. Well, hold on because I will probably lose some with what I say next. It starts to seem as if you are dealing with Dr. Jekyll and Mr. Hyde. And in truth you are.

One of the ways addicts in recovery often explain the experience of being caught in the grips of addiction is with the example of Dr. Jekyll and Mr. Hyde. This is one of the only ways to give someone who is not an addict some type of understanding of what it was like for us being in active addiction. The active side of our addiction is a beast. It is not as if your child is not still in there. They just can't come out as often the further they go into their addiction. I am in tears right now as I right as I remember being like Dr. Jekyll crying down on the inside as the beast (addiction) took over and ran wild in the lives of my loved ones. It was not as if I could not see the pain in my mother's eyes. I just was not at liberty at the time to do anything about it. The further we go in our addiction the less we care. The beast is obsessive, compulsive, self-centered and will hurt anyone in the way of getting and finding ways and means to get the next one. The beast was also cunning and able to beguile because it resembles me and had control of my person so it used this to play on sympathy.

You see the addiction will have your child come to you with those puppy dog eyes and pull on your sentiment. How can you resist your own child? If that doesn't work the addiction will tell your child to go to extremes such as hurting themselves in your presence or threatening to harm themselves if you don't give them what they want. This is one of the trump cards of the addiction. It has your child as a hostage and dangles them in your face threatening to do God awful things if you the parent won't comply. Back to the question, how can you resist your own child? You do so by seeing the illness of addiction for what it is. You do so by understanding you are saying no Mr. Hyde, not your child. You do so by looking the addiction square in the eyes and saying I see you for what you are and I will not become your slave, enabler, or victim (see figure 1). **You do this by loving your addicted child enough and hating the addiction enough to say "no" and "enough is enough".**

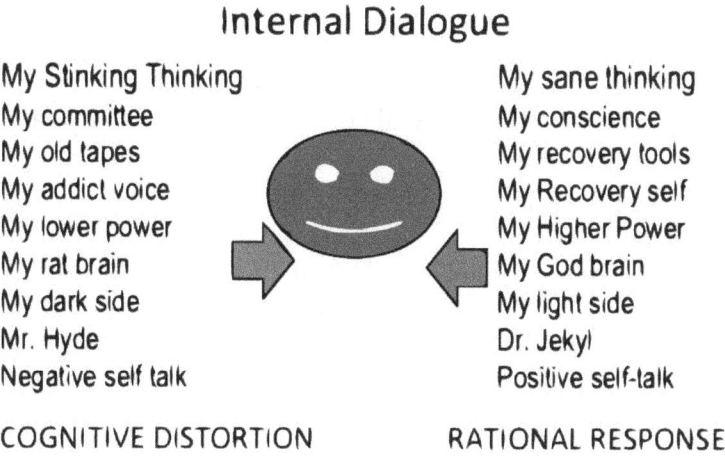

Internal Dialogue

My Stinking Thinking	My sane thinking
My committee	My conscience
My old tapes	My recovery tools
My addict voice	My Recovery self
My lower power	My Higher Power
My rat brain	My God brain
My dark side	My light side
Mr. Hyde	Dr. Jekyl
Negative self talk	Positive self-talk
COGNITIVE DISTORTION	RATIONAL RESPONSE

[Figure 1]

Some of us are Sicker than Others

In this section I will be referring to an aspect of addiction which will necessitate that I reference various experts in the field of addiction. It may seem at times a little more on the medical side, but I believe these things needs to be articulated in a manner that your addicted child may be unable to. What I will cover in this section is what some call dual diagnosis and co-occurring disorders. For instance, I was dual diagnosed when I was in my active addiction. I was diagnosed with a Substance Use Disorder (SUD) and clinical depression with acute anxiety. At one time I as a teenager I was also diagnosed and treated for Alcohol Use Disorder (AUD) and bipolar disorder. Some of you parents reading this have children who suffer from conditions that are co-occurring or bilateral such as AUD and depression (Doweiko, 2015). As The AA member – Medications & Other Drugs pamphlet states "Some of us have had to cope with depressions that can be suicidal;

schizophrenia that sometimes requires hospitalization;

manic depression; and other mental and biological

illnesses".

The reason I go into this is because for a parent it

can be confusing and frustrating to see your child suffering

and not have a clue as to what is the cause or underlying

issues. It helps when you are armed with knowledge as to

what is ailing your addicted child. This may not resolve the

problem, but it does offer hope that help is available, and

treatment is possible. I also write this because I was sicker

than most and I can attest to the fact that sometimes it is

confusing and frustrating to treating physicians and

professionals trying to properly assess , diagnose and treat

addicts with a co-occurring metal health issue. Again I refer

to Doweiko (2015) who states that diagnosing substance

abusers with concurrent depression is complicated as the

substance abuse can make the depression worse and

counter act the medication used to treat the secondary issue.

Doctors also often have to work through the dishonesty of the addicted child during assessments which make it hard to determine which condition is the primary or root issue.

So where does that leave you as a parent? In the remaining part of this section, I will suggest some practical steps you can take being armed with the information I shared above. These are in no real particular order as to level of importance, in my opinion, they are all equally valuable and help you in two ways. First, you will gain more knowledge as to what your addicted child's underlying issues are. Second, once your child is open to accepting or seeking help, you will be armed with knowledge that can help you point them in the right direction. So here is "What you can do":

1. **Do more Research** – It is vital that you don't just stop at the small amount of information I have provided or what you currently know. One of the first things the

addicted child will say to get a parent off their back is, "you just don't understand addiction". This is true for many parents. They try the best they can with what information they have and try to help us. But it is very important that as parents you arm yourselves with up-to-date information on your child's addiction and possible dual diagnosis. Here are a couple of terms that may help you start your research: Substance Use Disorder, Alcohol Use Disorder, Dual Diagnosis, Co-occurring disorders, Substance-Induced Mood Disorder, and DSM-5.

2. **Do Support Groups-** One of the awesome things available to parents of addicted children is the growing network of support. There has long been a population of those

who meet regularly and support each other in the form of groups such as Al-Anon. These are meetings where parents and loved ones share their experience, strength, and hope. It is also a safe place to share what you are trying to cope with. <u>Many times there are others who have gone through what you are experiencing and have gotten to the other side</u>. You will get information on things that worked for other parents as well as tap into a well of resources you might not hear about anywhere else.

However, there have been a growing number of online support groups. A simple search on google for "online support groups for parents of addicts" may yield some great findings. Also, if you are on Facebook just search the group section for addiction support groups, and you will find groups with thousands of parents supporting one another.

3. **Develop a Questionnaire-** This may sound strange, but it may be very handy when the time comes. There may come a time when your addicted child is sick and tired of being sick and tired. They are ready to come in from out in cold having been beaten to submission by addiction. They may come to you looking for a place to stay or a ride to the nearest treatment program. What would you do if that happened today? Would you have to scramble to find a good treatment program for your child? Or would you be armed with a list of potential facilities that can possibly help your child in her or his unique situation? I will provide a sample

questionnaire you can use when calling
potential treatment facilities or talking with
an intake counselor, or examining doctor.
This way you can have a list ready if and
when the day should ever arise that your
child comes to you for help after hitting rock
bottom.

Why Won't My Child Stop?

In this section, I will combine two questions. They are the questions many parents ask. **Why won't my child stop? And, when will enough be enough?** Some of these answers to these questions will be answered for parents who took my suggestions in the section above. I cannot stress how important it is to do your own research on addiction and substance abuse. There are many resources available, and I will offer some of them at the end of this book. There is a vast amount of research done on addiction and how to effectively treat it. There is no one size fit all approach to treating addiction.

This is because, with all the research and data that has been compiled, experts still are not in total agreement as to the terminology, treatment models, or even the diagnostic criteria of addiction. No consensus has emerged as to what the answer to addiction is (Ruiz, Strain, & Langrod, 2007). So if you ask 10 doctors, "why won't my child stop using?" you may get a different answer depending on that doctor's approach and the model of addiction they subscribe to. However, there are some aspects of addiction that are universally identifiable that contribute to why the addict continues to use regardless of the consequences.

The first is <u>the obsessive and compulsive nature of addiction</u>. As a recovering addict myself I can tell you what this is like. The obsession is such that all thoughts are tasked to find ways and means to get more drugs or alcohol. It is called being locked and loaded on a fixed idea. Being consumed with the thoughts of getting high, makes things such as common consideration of others impossible at times. As a parent I am sure you may have noticed that even the concern for personal hygiene and appearance takes a backseat to the addiction. This is one of the most enslaving aspects of addiction. Trying to carry a conversation with someone needing a fix will often go sideways because they are too fixed on getting high. I can remember seeing people's mouths moving but only thinking of getting my next fix. In this state of active addiction it is hard to talk to and nearly impossible to reason with the addicted child.

Here is an example of how the obsession works. An addict gets high all day. The addict overdoses or gets alcohol poisoning. The addict is in the hospital. Before the addict is out of the hospital gown they begin to think of where they can get more. The addict gets out of the hospital and goes straight to the place where they can pick up where they left off. The addict gets more drugs and alcohol and starts to use them. <u>Before the addict even finishes these substances they begin to contemplate ways to not run out.</u> This may sound crazy and far-fetched, but I was that addict in my active addiction. There are entire years of my life that were dictated by my obsession. Years went by where my sole mission was to find ways and means to get more drugs and alcohol.

The compulsion that addicts experience is best depicted in the saying, "One is too many, and a thousand is never enough." This is why **addicts have to abstain from all mood and mind altering substances** because words like "moderation" or phrases like "wean off" don't apply to us. Once we get "it" in us, we are off to the races. It can be any substance because addiction does not discriminate. This one of the main reasons why your addicted child may be struggling to stop and stay stopped. We can NOT substitute one drug for another. Many of us have tried to stop using one drug and just drink or stop drinking and just smoke marijuana. The compulsion that addicts battle daily is what many have referred to as being *"caught in the grips"*.

Another reason why an active addict won't stop has to do with shame and guilt. Shame and guilt often fuels the continued use of drugs and alcohol. This is not the healthy shame or feelings of remorse and guilt. The healthy guilt can cause a person to experience a level of sorrow that leads to a change. This is the shame and guilt that addicts deal with which attacks an already low to no self-esteem. It causes the addict to be unable to face themselves in the mirror. It is the type of crushing sense of utter worthlessness. This shame and guilt can beat the addict down worse than anything that any human can say. To cope with or escape these feelings the addict continues to use. The use of drugs helps numb these feelings temporarily. But after the numbness wares off the obsession and compulsion kick in. This is what is known as the vicious cycle of addiction. Once the addict is caught in this cycle, it often takes hitting rock bottom to stop.

Parents I hope you are beginning to understand what your child is actually unable to express. There is an continual inner turmoil that has to be quieted. There are moments of sobriety that seem tortuous at times for an addict. When we sober up and have to deal with what we have done and who we have become it is hard to live with ourselves without self-medicating. This is in no way condoning any aspect of our behavior during active addiction. I am just trying to give you an honest firsthand account of what your child is battling with. It is my hope that this will help you to better understand the *"why"*.

So when is enough going to be enough? I often hear parents ask, "Why doesn't my child just quit seeing how bad things are". Two things are at work. First the very essence and medical definition of addiction is continued use despite the consequences. The term rock bottom also comes into play here. This term can be controversial. Some people swear that a person must hit rock bottom before they will quit. There is a great deal of truth to this statement. <u>But rock bottom is different for everyone</u>. Some people's threshold for pain is more than others. But one thing that seems to be consistent is that when the pain is great enough people seek help. Sadly some have lost their lives to this illness, and countless others are still suffering.

It is my belief that a person does not necessarily have to hit rock bottom. Some addicts stop before things are at their worst. When an addict becomes sick and tired of being sick and tired, they often will seek help. Sometimes it takes the loss of someone or a jarring experience. Other times an intervention may help. Some have been mandated to treatment by the courts which turned out to be life changing. Ultimately, there is no one answer to when it will be enough for the addict. As stated above, one of the criteria for being an addict is that a person will continue to use regardless of what they lose, the damage it does, and how negatively it impacts their lives. Hopefully, I have shed a little light on the *"why"* in efforts to help you as parents to understand what it means to be caught in the grips of addiction. When you see these aspects of addiction playing out in the life of your child, you are now armed

with more understanding. Understanding goes a long way

for an addict. Trust me. But more importantly I trust that

such an understanding will help parents better address their

situation and support the addicted loved one.

WE DO RECOVER

I would like to close by sharing my experience, strength, and hope. While this is not my complete story, I pray it will bless some parent today. I was born in 1978 in Tidewater, VA. I came up in a two parent home. We were what some consider middle class. And for all intents and purposes, I believe I came up in a good but not perfect home. My mother has always been a godly Christian woman who walked out her faith as long as I can remember. My father who is a minister now was an alcoholic in those days. It was during my youth that I had my first encounter with what understand today to be a family disease.

I remember going to AlaTeen and AlaNon when I was around 12 years old. We had done interventions on my father for his alcoholism. Little did I know one day I would be in the same place in the same seat having an intervention done on me. As I got older, I began to experiment with drugs and alcohol. I first started drinking in the 5th grade.

By the time I was in 6th grade, I was having black outs from drinking. By the end of high school, I had been hospitalized for drinking, expelled for drug-related issues, and in and out of treatment facilities.

I joined the Navy after high school. I was later discharged for failure to rehabilitate on Alcohol. My drinking and drugging had taken over and ruined my life. I ended up having gone through every type of treatment program from in-patient to outpatient both short and long term. I was diagnosed and treated for a dual diagnosis. I was placed in numerous mental institutions. I was arrested on several occasion and taken to jail. I had tried AA and NA and never took it too serious. My family worried and suffered because of my addiction.

One day I was at the mental institution and a counselor recommended I go into a yearlong faith based inpatient treatment facility away from home. I did. I ended up completing the program successfully and becoming a part of staff. I earned my first associates degree and became a Chaplin at the program. I accepted my calling to preach and felt led to go into counseling. I stayed clean and sober over 2 years that time before I moved back home. When my uncle died, I used that as an excuse to use, and I relapsed. That relapse was the worst one of them all. I could not get high, and things just did not feel the same. No matter how much I drank I didn't feel anything. For what seemed to be the longest months of my life I struggled with falling so far after years of sobriety, recovery, and ministry.

Shortly after meeting my soon to be wife, I checked myself into yet another program. This time, I put into practice all the things I had been taught before. I had become sick and tired of being sick and tired. I completed that program. Continued aftercare and went to meetings, got a sponsor, and worked the 12 steps. I ended up in a sober living house and started becoming a productive member of society. I continued going to church, meetings, and taking suggestions of those in recovery.

Today by the grace of God I celebrate being over 13 years sober and drug-free. I am married with 2 beautiful children. I have been blessed to have earned my MA in Addictions Counseling from Liberty University. I also, co-host the *Recovery Just for Today* radio show with my father. Which is a show dedicated to those suffering from addiction and their family members. This is my second book to help those impacted by addiction. As a counselor it is my ethical duty to suggest that parents get some outside help. Tools such as this book and other materials are awesome helps. But I STRONGLY suggest seeking professional help and finding support groups in your area. There is much more I can share about my journey. I am truly grateful today. I want parents to know if it happened for me it can for your child. There is still hope. WE DO RECOVER!!!!

SAMPLE QUESTIONAIRRE

FOR THE PROFESSIONAL HELPER

1. What are my child's diagnoses? And what does the DSM-5 Diagnostic and Statistical Manual of Mental Disorders, Fifth Edition say?

2. What can you tell me about this diagnosis?

3. Have you ruled out a dual diagnosis?

4. Are there any underlying issues or secondary conditions that we need to know of?

5. What is your suggested treatment plan? Do you have any relapse prevention resources?

6. Do you use an integrated treatment approach? And can you recommend any support groups and family support groups?

7 MUST HAVE RESOURCES

1.   http://al-anon.org/ Friends and families of problem drinkers find understanding and support at Al-Anon

2.   http://www.nar-anon.org/ Friends and families of addicts find understanding and support at Narconon

3.   http://www.addictionrecoveryguide.org/ A messages board with many resources

4.   https://www.ncadd.org/family-friends/there-is-help/family-disease National Recovery Support and Advocacy

5.   http://www.samhsa.gov/find-help/national-helpline SAMHSA's National Helpline is a free, confidential, 24/7, 365-day-a-year treatment referral and information service (in English and Spanish) for individuals and families facing mental health and/or substance use disorders.

6. http://freeaddictionhotline.com/integrated-treatment/ Also has a help line but this link can explain integrated treatment

7. **Christian Recovery Centers** Recovery.org has many resources and has information on faith-based programs and support

THE 30 DAY

CHALLENGE

For the next thirty days, I challenge you to put into practice what was discussed in this book. It is not enough to just read without putting these new concepts and principles into action. So for the next 30 days, I challenge you to use the included journal to write about your experience. This is an exercise that can be used long after the pages in this book have been used up. I would suggest taking this challenge soon after reading the book and not to procrastinate.

This is how the Challenge Works.

1. Week 1 you will focus on the using the Serenity Prayer. At the end of each day, you will write in your journal about what the Serenity Prayer means to you and how you used it and why.

2. Week 2 you will focus on Acceptance. At the end of each day, you will write in your journal about what acceptance means to you and how you used it and why.

3. Week 3 you will focus on Courage. At the end of each day, you will write in your journal about what Courage means to you and how you used it and why.

4. Week 4 you will focus on Wisdom. At the end of each day, you will write in your journal about what Wisdom means to you and how you used it and why.

Make sure to include setbacks and how you reacted to situations as you attempted to put these principles into action. Write about what you want to better the next day and end of each night with the serenity prayer. Also during this week meditate on the complete version of the Serenity Prayer found on the next page.

The Serenity Prayer

by Reinhold Niebuhr (1892-1971)
Complete, Unabridged, Original Version.

God, give us grace to accept with serenity

the things that cannot be changed,

Courage to change the things

which should be changed,

and the Wisdom to distinguish

the one from the other.

Living one day at a time,

Enjoying one moment at a time,

Accepting hardship as a pathway to peace,

Taking, as Jesus did,

This sinful world as it is,

Not as I would have it,

Trusting that You will make all things right,

If I surrender to Your will,

So that I may be reasonably happy in this life,

And supremely happy with You forever in the next.

Amen.

Week1 Day 1

Focus on the using the Serenity Prayer. At the end of each day you will write in your journal about what the Serenity Prayer means to you and how you used it and why.

Week1 Day 2

Focus on the using the Serenity Prayer. At the end of each day you will write in your journal about what the Serenity Prayer means to you and how you used it and why.

Week1 Day 3

Focus on the using the Serenity Prayer. At the end of each day you will write in your journal about what the Serenity Prayer means to you and how you used it and why.

Week1 Day 4

Focus on the using the Serenity Prayer. At the end of each day you will write in your journal about what the Serenity Prayer means to you and how you used it and why.

Week1 Day 5

Focus on the using the Serenity Prayer. At the end of each day you will write in your journal about what the Serenity Prayer means to you and how you used it and why.

Week1 Day 6

Focus on the using the Serenity Prayer. At the end of each day you will write in your journal about what the Serenity Prayer means to you and how you used it and why.

Week1 Day 7

Focus on the using the Serenity Prayer. At the end of each day you will write in your journal about what the Serenity Prayer means to you and how you used it and why.

Week2 Day 1

Focus on Acceptance. At the end of each day you will write in your journal about what acceptance means to you and how you used it and why

Week2 Day2

Focus on Acceptance. At the end of each day you will write in your journal about what acceptance means to you and how you used it and why

Week2 Day 3

Focus on Acceptance. At the end of each day you will write in your journal about what acceptance means to you and how you used it and why

Week2 day 4

Focus on Acceptance. At the end of each day you will write in your journal about what acceptance means to you and how you used it and why

Week2 Day 5

Focus on Acceptance. At the end of each day you will write in your journal about what acceptance means to you and how you used it and why

Week2 Day 6

Focus on Acceptance. At the end of each day you will write in your journal about what acceptance means to you and how you used it and why

Week2 Day 7

Focus on Acceptance. At the end of each day you will write in your journal about what acceptance means to you and how you used it and why

Week3 Day 1

Focus on Courage. At the end of each day you will write in your journal about what Courage means to you and how you used it and why.

Week3 Day 2

Focus on Courage. At the end of each day you will write in your journal about what Courage means to you and how you used it and why.

Week3 Day 3

Focus on Courage. At the end of each day you will write in your journal about what Courage means to you and how you used it and why.

Week3 Day 4

Focus on Courage. At the end of each day you will write in your journal about what Courage means to you and how you used it and why.

Week3 Day 5

Focus on Courage. At the end of each day you will write in your journal about what Courage means to you and how you used it and why.

Week3 Day 6

Focus on Courage. At the end of each day you will write in your journal about what Courage means to you and how you used it and why.

Week3 Day 7

Focus on Courage. At the end of each day you will write in your journal about what Courage means to you and how you used it and why.

Week 4 Day 1

Focus on Wisdom. At the end of each day you will write in your journal about what Wisdom means to you and how you used it and why.

Week 4 Day 2

Focus on Wisdom. At the end of each day you will write in your journal about what Wisdom means to you and how you used it and why.

Week 4 Day 3

Focus on Wisdom. At the end of each day you will write in your journal about what Wisdom means to you and how you used it and why.

Week 4 Day 4

Focus on Wisdom. At the end of each day you will write in your journal about what Wisdom means to you and how you used it and why.

Week 4 Day 5

Focus on Wisdom. At the end of each day you will write in your journal about what Wisdom means to you and how you used it and why.

Week 4 Day 6

Focus on Wisdom. At the end of each day you will write in your journal about what Wisdom means to you and how you used it and why.

Week 4 Day 7

Focus on Wisdom. At the end of each day you will write in your journal about what Wisdom means to you and how you used it and why.

The Lord's Prayer

Matthew 6:9-13New International Version (NIV)

[9] "This, then, is how you should pray:

"'Our Father in heaven,

hallowed be your name,

[10] your kingdom come,

your will be done,

   on earth as it is in heaven.

[11] Give us today our daily bread.

[12] And forgive us our debts,

   as we also have forgiven our debtors.

[13] And lead us not into temptation,[a]

   but deliver us from the evil one.[b]'

The Lord is my Shepherd

Psalm 2321st Century King James Version (KJ21)

23 The Lord is my shepherd; I shall not want.

[2] He maketh me to lie down in green pastures; He leadeth me beside the still waters.

[3] He restoreth my soul; He leadeth me in the paths of righteousness for His name's sake.

[4] Yea, though I walk through the valley of the shadow of death, I will fear no evil; for Thou art with me; Thy rod and Thy staff, they comfort me.

[5] Thou preparest a table before me in the presence of mine enemies; Thou anointest my head with oil; my cup runneth over.

[6] Surely goodness and mercy shall follow me all the days of my life; and I will dwell in the house of the Lord for ever.

ADDICTION TERMS

- Alkaloids: Plant-produced organic compounds that are the active ingredients in many drugs

- Amphetamine: A behavioral stimulant; also known as pep pills

- Analgesic: Medication designed to treat pain

- Antagonist: A substance that can nullify another's effects (a drug that does not elicit a response)

- AOD: Stands for (Alcohol and Other Drugs)

- AODA: Stands for (Alcohol and Other Drug Abuse)

- Aspirin: An anti-inflammatory agent used for pain relief

- Barbiturate: A class of sedative-hypnotic compounds that are chemically related through a six-membered ring structure

- Benzodiazepine: A group of depressants used to induce sleep, prevent seizures, produce sedation, relieve anxiety and muscle

- Bioavailability: A drug's ability to enter the body
- Biofeedback: Signal use to control physiological processes that are normally involuntary
- Blood Alcohol Level/Concentration: The concentration level of alcohol in the bloodstream (expressed as a percentage by weight)
- Buprenorphine: A semi-synthetic partial agonist opioid derived from the baine; used for pain relief (e.g. Buprenex)
- Caffeine: An alkaloid that acts as a diuretic and a stimulant (found in coffee, tea, etc.)
- Carcinogen: A cancer-causing chemical agent
- Causal Factors: Various antecedent conditions that lead to individual chemical dependency problems (e.g. conditioning, environment, genetics, etc.)
- Ceiling Effect: Occurs when the dosage of buprenorphine is increased beyond maximum levels and no differences result

- Center for Substance Abuse Treatment (CSAT): Promotes community-based substance abuse treatment services

- Central Nervous System (CNS): The brain and spinal cord

- Certified Chemical Dependency Counselor (CCDC): Manages clients in chemical dependency programs to help with addiction recovery

- Cirrhosis: Chronic liver disease

- Clinical Opiate Withdrawal Scale (COWS): Used to determine the severity of opioid withdrawal

- Codeine: The pain-relieving sedative agent contained in opium

- Codependence: A family member's or friend's suffering that is the result of the side effects of one's addiction; it occurs when one takes responsibility for another's actions and helps that person avoid facing his or her problems directly to maintain the relationship

- Cold Turkey: Abruptly quitting a drug by choice in order to try to quit long-term
- Compulsion: A physical behavior one repeats involuntarily that can be harmful (e.g., addiction)
- Conditioning: A behavioral change that results from an association between events
- Craving: A powerful and strong desire/urge for a substance; a symptom of the abnormal brain adaptions that result from addiction
- Crisis Intervention: The action taken when one's usual coping resources pose a threat to individual or family functioning
- Cross-Dependence: The ability of one drug to prevent the withdrawal symptoms of one's physical dependence on another

- Cross-Tolerance: Occurs when one's tolerance for one drug results in their lessened response to another

- D.O.C.: This stands for drug of choice.

- Denial: One's failure to either admit or realize his or her addiction or to recognize and accept the harm it can cause

- Depressants: Sedatives that act on the CNS (e.g. to treat anxiety, high blood pressure, tension, etc.)

- Depression: One of the most frequent types of distress resulting from addiction; an ongoing state of sadness involving the inability to concentrate, inactivity, etc.

- Detoxification (Detox): The process of removing a toxic substance (e.g. a drug) from the body

- Disease Model: A theory of alcoholism that considers the addiction a disease rather than a social or psychological issue.

- Disease: A condition featuring medically significant symptoms that often have a known cause

- Doctor Shopping: Occurs when a patient requests care simultaneously from multiple physicians without their knowledge in order to receive higher amounts of medications

- Dopamine: A chemical produced naturally by the body; functions in the brain as a neurotransmitter to provide feelings of well-being

- Downers: Another name for depressants; these drugs can cause low moods (e.g. alcohol, barbiturates, tranquilizers, etc.)

- Drug Misuse: One's use of a drug not specifically recommended or prescribed when there are more practical alternatives; when drug use puts a user or others in danger

- Drug Tolerance: A progressive state of decreased responsiveness to a drug

- DSM-IV: The handbook most often used for diagnosing mental disorders

- Dual-Diagnosis: Mental patients ' condition when they are also addicted to any mind-altering drug

- DUI: Stands for (driving under influence) (of alcohol or another illicit substance that impairs one's ability to drive)

- DWI: Stands for (driving while intoxicated)

- Dysphoria: The opposite of euphoria

- Dysynergy: An addiction's tendency to cause another (e.g. gateway drugs); an addicted person's tendency to combine substances

- Enabling: Helping an addicted person do things they can or should be doing for themselves; causes disease progression

- Endogenous Opioid: The opioids that the body naturally produces in order to help us tolerate pain

- Endorphins: Opium-like substances produced by the brain; natural painkillers

- Ethanol: The beverage type (ethyl) of alcohol

- Euphoria: A pleasurable state of altered consciousness; one reason for the preference of one addictive behavior or substance over another

- Evidence-based Treatment: Scientifically validated treatment approaches

- Excipient: An inactive substance added to a drug to help bind the active ingredient

- Fetal Alcohol Syndrome (FAS): Birth defects/abnormalities in babies of alcoholic and alcohol abusing mothers

- Fetal Drug Syndrome (FDS): Birth defects/abnormalities in babies of drug abusing mothers

- Food and Drug Administration (FDA): Administers federal laws regarding, for example, the safety and effectiveness of drugs

- Habit: An outdated term for addiction/physical dependence

- Hallucinogen: Chemical substance that distorts perceptions, sometimes resulting in delusions or hallucinations

- Harm Reduction: Often the first stage of addiction treatment; reducing therapy instead of stopping the target behavior

- Heroin: A full opioid agonist

- Hydrocodone: An effective narcotic analgesic first developed as a cough medication

- Addiction Illegal/Illicit Drugs: Drugs that are illegal to produce, use, and sell

- Induction: Beginning phase of buprenorphine treatment

- Inflation: An addiction behavior's tendency to slowly but surely increase in frequency

- Intoxication: A state of being drugged or poisoned; results from abuse of alcohol, barbiturates, toxic drugs, etc.

- Intrinsic Activity: The extent to which a drug activates a receptor

- Legal Drugs: Everyday drugs not for medical use (e.g. alcohol, caffeine, carbohydrates, nicotine, etc.)

- Maintenance: Stabilization of a patient who is indefinitely on a drug's lowest effective dose

- Medical Model: An addiction theory that considers addiction a medical rather than social issue

- Metabolism (of drugs): The chemical and physical reactions carried out by the body to prepare for a drug's execution

- Methadone: A long-acting opiate (synthetically produced)

- Monotherapy: Therapy using one drug

- Morphine: A major sedative/pain reliever found in opium

- Mu Agonist: A drug that stimulates physiologic activity on mu opioid cell receptors

- Mu Opioid Receptor: Nerve cell receptor that mediates opioid addiction and tolerance through drug-induced activity

- Naloxone: An opioid antagonist that blocks the effects of opioid agonists

- Naltrexone: A narcotic antagonist that blocks the effects of opioids

- Narcotic: A drug that produces sleep/drowsiness and that also relieves pain while being potentially dependence producing

- National Board of Addiction Examiners (NBAE): Provides certification for individuals in the addiction field

- Negative Reinforcement: Repetitive behavior to avoid something unpleasant

- Neurotransmitter: The natural chemical a neuron releases to communicate with or influence another

- Nicotine: Tobacco's extremely toxic main active ingredient (causes negative CNS stimulation)

- Nonopioid: A drug that doesn't activate opioid receptors

- Obsession: A mental behavior one repeats involuntarily that can be harmful (e.g., (needing) an alcoholic drink)

- Off-Label Use: Physician-approved use of a drug for uses other than those stated on its label

- Opiate: The poppy's natural ingredients and their derivatives (opium, morphine, codeine, and heroin)

- Opioids: Opium's synthetic form

- Opium: One of the most popular drugs; contained in muscle-relaxers, sleeping pills, and tranquilizers

- Over-the-Counter Drugs: Legal non-prescription drugs

- Oxycodone: A medicine used for relief of moderate to high pain

- Painkillers: Analgesic substances (opioids and non-opioids)

- Partial Agonists: Bind to and activate receptors to a lesser degree than full agonists

- Pharmacology: Scientific branch dealing with the study of drugs and their actions

- Physical Dependence: The body's physiologic adaptation to a substance

- Placebo: A substance with no pharmacological elements that may elicit a reaction because of a patient's mindset

- Polysubstance Abuse: Concurrent abuse of more than one substance

- Post-Acute Withdrawal Syndrome (PAWS): Withdrawal symptoms after initial acute withdrawal

- Precipitated Withdrawal Syndrome: Can occur when a patient on full-agonist opioids takes an antagonist

- Prescription Drugs: Only available by a physician's order

- Psychedelic Drugs: Produce an intensely pleasurable mental state

- Psychoactive Drug: A mind- and behavior-altering substance

- Psychological Dependence: One's compulsion to use a psychologically based drug for pleasure; may lead to drug misuse

- Psychopharmacology: The study of how drugs affect consciousness, mood, sensation, etc.

- Psychotropic Drug: Any drug that acts on one's psychic experience or mood behavior

- Rapid Detox: Anesthesia-assisted detoxification (injection of high doses of an opiate antagonist, followed by an infusion of naloxone)

- Receptor: Protein on a target cell's membrane or cytoplasm with which a drug interacts

- Recidivism: One's return to a negative behavior (relapse) (e.g. drug use)

- Recovery Rates: The percentage of addicted persons undergoing treatment who partake in abstinence in their first year

- Recovery: Reducing or ceasing substance abuse; often followed by one's personal life being turned around by way of a supportive environment

- Relapse Prevention: A therapeutic process that interrupts believes and behaviors that result in lifestyle dysfunction

- Relapse: Symptom recurrence after a period of sobriety or drug use cessation

- Remission: A symptom-free period

- Reversed Tolerance: When a lower dose of a drug produces the same desired or observed effect that previously resulted only with higher dosages

- Screening: Measurement tool for the extent of one's addiction (e.g., self-completion questionnaire/life-history assessment)

- Self-Help Group: Group of individuals dealing with similar issues that meets to support each other and share helpful information (e.g. AA)

- Side Effects: Secondary effects of a drug; these are usually undesirable

- Societal Denial: Society's denial of the historical value of drug-induced pleasure and euphoria

- Steroids: A group of cyclic, solid unsaturated alcohols (e.g. cholesterol)

- Stimulant: Drugs that act on the CNS, resulting in alertness, excitation, and wakefulness

- Straight-Edge: A term for people who don 't use drugs

- Sublingual: Drugs that enter the blood through the membranes under the tongue

- Substance Abuse (Chemical Dependence): A maladaptive pattern of recurrent substance use that leads to impairment or distress that is clinically significant

- Substance Dependence:

- Synergism: The greater effect that results when one takes more than one drug simultaneously

- Synthetic: Not natural occurring

- Talc Granulomatosis:

- Talc: Dangerous substance used in manufacturing pharmaceuticals

- Therapeutic Community: A setting where people with similar issues can meet to support each other's recovery

- Therapeutic Dependence: Patients ' tendency to demonstrate drug-seeking behaviors because they fear withdrawal symptoms

- Titration: The gradual adjustment of the amount of a drug

- Tolerance: Condition in which one must increase their use of a drug for it to have the same effect

- Toxicity: A degree of poisonousness

- Tranquilizers: A type of drug that can help relieve the symptoms of severe psychosis

- Trigger: Anything that results in psychological and then physical relapse

- Ups or Uppers: Drugs that produce a euphoric effect (e.g. stimulants, amphetamines)

- Urge-Peak Cycle: Ongoing urge-peaks, usually followed by relapse

- Urge-Peak: A sudden, unpredictable increase in addiction cravings; they usually involve temporary mental unawareness (e.g. not realizing the amount of drinks one has had)

- Urges: Less powerful desires than cravings; can be suppressed by willpower

- User: Outdated term used to describe one who misuses alcohol or drugs

- Withdrawal Symptoms: Severe and excruciating physical and emotional symptoms that generally occur between 4 to 72 hours after opiate withdrawal (e.g., watery eyes, yawning, loss of appetite, panic, insomnia, vomiting, shaking, irritability, jitters, etc.)

- Withdrawal Syndrome: Combined reactions or behaviors that result from the abrupt cessation of a drug one is dependent on

- Withdrawal: The abrupt decrease in or removal of one's regular dosage of a psychoactive substance

STREET DRUG TERMONOLOGY

Alphabetical Listing

A - LSD; amphetamine

Abe - $5 worth of drugs

Abe's cabe - $5 bill

Abolic - veterinary steroid

Acapulco gold - marijuana from S.W.Mexico

Acapulco red - marijuana

Ace - marijuana; PCP

Acid - LSD

Acid cube - sugar cube containing LSD

Acid freak - heavy user of LSD

Acid head - LSD user

AD - PCP

Adam - MDMA

African black - marijuana

African bush - marijuana

African woodbine - marijuana cigarette

Agonies - withdrawal symptoms

Ah-pen-yen - opium

Aimies - amphetamine; amyl nitrite

AIP - heroin from Afghanistan, Iran, & Pakistan

Air blast - inhalant

Airhead - marijuana user

Airplane - marijuana

Alice B. Toklas - marijuana brownie

All lit up - under the influence of drugs

All star - user of multiple drugs

All-American drug - cocaine

Alpha-ET - alpha-ethyltyptamine

Ames - amyl nitrite

Amidone - methadone

Amoeba - PCP

Amp - amphetamine

Amp joint - marijuana cigarette laced with some form of narcotic

Amped-out - fatigue after using amphetamines

Amping - accelerated heartbeat

AMT - dimethyltryptamine

Amys - amyl nitrate

Anadrol - oral steroid

Anatrofin - injectable steroid

Anavar - oral steroid

Angel - PCP

Angel dust - PCP

Angel hair - PCP

Angel mist - PCP

Angel Poke - PCP

Angie - cocaine

Angola - marijuana

Animal - LSD

Animal tranq - PCP

Animal tranquilizer - PCP

Antifreeze - heroin

Apache - fentanyl

Apple jacks - crack

Aries - heroin

Aroma of men - isobutyl nitrite

Artillery - equipment for injecting drugs

Ashes - marijuana

Astro turf - marijuana

Atom bomb - marijuana and heroin

Atshitshi - marijuana

Aunt Hazel - heroin

Aunt Mary - marijuana

Aunt Nora - cocaine

Aunti - opium

Aunti Emma - opium

Aurora borealis - PCP

Author - a doctor who writes illegal prescriptions

B - amount of marijuana to fill a matchbox

B-bombs - amphetamines

B-40 - cigar laced with marijuana and dipped in malt liquor

B.J.'s - crack

Babe - drug used for detoxification

Baby - marijuana

Baby bhang - marijuana

Baby habit - occasional use of drugs

Babysit - guide someone through first drug experience

Baby T - crack

Backbreakers - LSD and strychnine

Back door - residue left in a pipe

Backjack - injecting opium

Back to back - smoking crack after injecting heroin or
heroin used after smoking crack

Backtrack - allow blood to flow back into a needle during
injection

Backup - prepare vein for injection

Backwards - depressant

Bad bundle - inferior quality heroin

Bad - crack

Bad go - bad reaction to a drug

Bad seed - peyote; heroin; marijuana

Bag - container for drugs

Bag bride - crack-smoking prostitute

Bag man - person who transports money

Bagging - using inhalant

Bale - marijuana

Ball - crack

Balling - vaginally implanted cocaine

Balloon - heroin supplier

Ballot - heroin

Bam - depressant; amphetamine

Bambalacha - marijuana

Bambs - depressant

Bang - to inject a drug; inhalant

Bank bandit pills - depressant

Bar - marijuana

Barb - depressant

Barbies - depressant

Barbs - cocaine

Barrels - LSD

Bart Simpson - heroin

Base - cocaine; crack

Baseball - crack

Base crazies - searching on hands and knees for crack

Base head - person who bases

Bash - marijuana

Basuco - cocaine; coca paste residue sprinkled on marijuana or regular cigarette

Bathtub speed - methcathinone

Batt - IV needle

Battery acid - LSD

Batu - smokable methamphetamine

Bazooka - cocaine; crack; crack and tobacco combined in a joint

Bazulco - cocaine

Beam me up Scottie - crack dipped in PCP

Beamer - crack user

Beans - amphetamine; depressant; mescaline

Beast - LSD

Beat artist - person selling bogus drugs

Beat vials - vials containing sham crack to cheat buyers

Beautiful boulders - crack

Bevis & Butthead - LSD

Bebe - crack

Bedbugs - fellow addicts

Beedies - cigarettes from India (resemble marijuana joints/vehicles for other drugs)

Beemers - crack

Behind the scale - to weigh and sell cocaine

Beiging - chemicals altering cocaine to make it appear a higher purity

Belladonna - PCP

Belt - effects of drugs

Belushi - cocaine and heroin

Belyando spruce - marijuana

Bender - drug party

Bennie - amphetamine

Bens - amphetamine

Benz - amphetamine

Benzedrine - amphetamine

Bernice - cocaine

Bernie - cocaine

Bernie's flakes - cocaine

Bernie's gold dust - cocaine

Bhang - marijuana, Indian term

Big bag - heroin

Big bloke - cocaine

Big C - cocaine

Big 8 - 1/8 kilogram of crack

Big D - LSD

Big H - heroin

Big Harry - heroin

Big flake - cocaine

Big man - drug supplier

Big O - opium

Big rush - cocaine

Bill Blass - crack

Billie hoke - cocaine

Biker's coffee - methamphetamine and coffee

Bindle - small packet of drug powder; heroin

Bing - enough of a drug for one injection

Bingers - crack addicts

Bingo - to inject a drug

Bings - crack

Biphetamine - amphetamine

Bird head - LSD

Birdie powder - heroin; cocaine

Biscuit - 50 rocks of crack

Bite one's lips - to smoke marijuana

Biz - bag or portion of drugs

Black - opium; marijuana

Black acid - LSD; LSD and PCP

Black and white - amphetamine

Black bart - marijuana

Black beauties - depressant; amphetamine

Black birds - amphetamine

Black bombers - amphetamine

Black dust - PCP

Black ganga - marijuana resin

Black gold - high potency marijuana

Black gungi - marijuana from India

Black gunion - marijuana

Black hash - opium and hashish

Black mo/black moat - highly potent marijuana

Black mollies - amphetamine

Black mote - marijuana mixed with honey

Black pearl - heroin

Black pill - opium pill

Black rock - crack

Black Russian - hashish mixed with opium

Black star - LSD

Black stuff - heroin

Black sunshine - LSD

Black tabs - LSD

Black tar - heroin

Black whack - PCP

Blacks - amphetamine

Blanco - heroin

Blanket - marijuana cigarette

Blanks - low quality drugs

Blast - to smoke marijuana; to smoke crack

Blast a joint - to smoke marijuana

Blast a roach - to smoke marijuana

Blast a stick - to smoke marijuana

Blasted - under the influence of drugs

Blizzard - white cloud in a pipe used to smoke cocaine

Block - marijuana

Block busters - depressant

Blonde - marijuana

Blotter - LSD; cocaine

Blotter acid - LSD

Blotter cube - LSD

Blow - cocaine; to inhale cocaine; to smoke marijuana

Blow a fix - injection misses the vein and is wasted in the skin

blow a shot - injection misses the vein and is wasted in the skin

blow the vein - injection misses the vein and is wasted in the skin

Blow a stick - to smoke marijuana

Blow blue - to inhale cocaine

Blowcaine - crack diluted with cocaine

Blow coke - to inhale cocaine

Blow one's roof - to smoke marijuana

Blow smoke - to inhale cocaine

Blowing smoke - marijuana

Blowout - crack

Blow up - crack cut with lidocaine to increase size, weight, and street value

Blows - heroin

Blue - depressant; crack

Blue acid - LSD

Blue angels - depressant

Blue barrels - LSD

Blue birds - depressant

Blue boy - amphetamine

Blue bullets - depressant

Blue caps - mescaline

Blue chairs - LSD

Blue cheers - LSD

Blue de hue - marijuana from Vietnam

Blue devil - depressant

Blue dolls - depressant

Blue heaven - LSD

Blue heavens - depressant

Blud madman - PCP

Blue microdot - LSD

Blue mist - LSD

Blue moons - LSD

Blue sage - marijuana

Blue sky blond - high potency marijuana from Columbia

Blue tips - depressant

Blue vials - LSD

Blunt - marijuana inside a cigar; marijuana and cocaine inside a cigar

Bo - marijuana

Bo-bo - marijuana

Boat - PCP

Bobo - crack

Bobo bush - marijuana

Body packer - person who ingests crack or cocaine to transport it

Body stuffer - person who ingests crack vials to avoid prosecution

Bogart a joint - salivate on a marijuana cigarette; refuse to share

Bohd - marijuana; PCP

Bolasterone - injectable steroid

Bolivian marching powder - cocaine

Bolo - crack

Bolt - isobutyl nitrite

Bomb - crack; heroin; large marijuana cigarette; high potency heroin

Bomb squad - crack-selling crew

Bomber - marijuana cigarette

Bombido - injectable amphetamine; heroin; depressant

Bombita - amphetamine; heroin; depressant

Bombs away - heroin

Bone - marijuana; $50 piece of crack

Bonecrusher - crack

Bones - crack

Bong - pipe used to smoke marijuana

Bonita - heroin

Boo - marijuana

Boom - marijuana

Boomers - psilocybin/psilocin

Boost - to inject a drug; to steal

Boost and shoot - steal to support a habit

Booster - to inhale cocaine

Boot - to inject a drug

Boot the gong - to smoke marijuana

Booted - under the influence of drugs

Boppers - amyl nitrite

Botray - crack

Bottles - crack vials; amphetamine

Boubou - crack

Boulder - crack; $20 worth of crack

Boulya - crack

Bouncing powder - cocaine

Boxed - in jail

Boy - heroin

Bozo - heroin

Brain damage - heroin

Brain ticklers - amphetamine

Breakdowns - $40 crack rock sold for $20

Break night - staying up all night until day break

Brewery - place where drugs are made

Brick - 1 kilogram of marijuana; crack

Brick gum - heroin

Bridge up or bring up - ready a vein for injection

Britton - peyote

Broccoli - marijuana

Broker - go-between in a drug deal

Bromo - 2C-B

Brown - heroin; marijuana

Brown bombers - LSD

Brown crystal - heroin

Brown dots - LSD

Brown rhine - heroin

Brown sugar - heroin

Brownies - amphetamine

Browns - amphetamine

Bubble gum - cocaine; crack

Buck - shoot someone in the head

Bud - marijuana

Buda - a high-grade marijuana joint filled with crack

Buffer - crack smoker; a woman who exchanges oral sex
for crack

Bugged - annoyed; to be covered with sores and abscesses
from repeated use of unsterile needles

Bull - narcotics agent or police officer

Bullet - isobutyl nitrite

Bullet bolt - inhalant

Bullia capital - crack

Bullion - crack

Bullyon - marijuana

Bumblebees - amphetamine

Bummer trip - unsettling and threatening experience from

PCP intoxication

Bump - crack; fake crack; boost a high; hit of ketamine

($20)

Bundle - heroin

Bunk - fake cocaine

Burese - cocaine

Burn one - to smoke marijuana

Burn the main line - to inject a drug

Burned - purchase fake drugs

Burned out - collapse of veins from repeated injection

permanent impairment from drug abuse

Burnese - cocaine

Burnie - marijuana

Burnout - heavy abuser of drugs

Bush - cocaine; marijuana

Businessman's LSD - dimethyltryptamine

Businessman's trip - dimethyltryptamine

Businessman's special - dimethyltryptamine

Busted - arrested

Busters - depressant

Busy bee - PCP

Butt naked - PCP

Butter - marijuana; crack

Butter flower - marijuana

Buttons - mescaline

Butu - heroin

Buzz - under the influence of drugs

Buzz bomb - nitrous oxide

C - Cocaine

C joint - place where cocaine is sold

C & M - cocaine and morphine

C.S. - marijuana

C-dust - cocaine

C-game - cocaine

Caballo - heroin

Cabello - cocaine

Caca - heroin

Cactus - mescaline

Cactus buttons - mescaline

Cactus head - mescaline

Cad/Cadillac - 1 ounce

Cadillac - PCP

Cadillac express - meth cathinone

Cakes - round discs of crack

Caine - cocaine; crack

California cornflakes - cocaine

California sunshine - LSD

Cam trip - high potency marijuana

Cambodian red/Cam red - marijuana from Cambodia

Came - cocaine

Can - marijuana; 1 ounce

Canadian black - marijuana

Canamo - marijuana

Canappa - marijuana

Cancelled stick - marijuana cigarette

Candy - cocaine; crack; depressant; amphetamine

Candy C - cocaine

Candy flipping - combining or sequencing LSD with

MDMA

Cannabinol - PCP

Cannabis tea - marijuana

Cap - crack; LSD

Caps - crack

Cap up - transfer bulk form drugs to capsules

Capital H - heroin

Caps - heroin; psilocybin/psilocin

Carburetor - crack stem attachment

Carga - heroin

Carmabis - marijuana

Carne - heroin

Carnie - cocaine

Carpet patrol - crack smokers searching the floor for crack

Carrie - cocaine

Carrie Nation - cocaine

Cartucho - package of marijuana cigarettes

Cartwheels - amphetamine

Casper the ghost - crack

Cat - meth cathinone

Cat valium - ketamine

Catnip - marijuana cigarette

Caviar - crack

Cavite all star - marijuana

Cecil - cocaine

Cest - marijuana

Chalk - methamphetamine; amphetamine

Chalked up - under the influence of cocaine

Chalking - chemically altering the color of cocaine so it looks white

Chandoo/chandu - opium

Channel - vein into which a drug is injected

Channel swimmer - one who injects heroin

Charas - marijuana from India

Charge - marijuana

Charged up - under the influence of drugs

Charley - heroin

Charlie - cocaine

Chase - to smoke cocaine; to smoke marijuana

Chaser - compulsive crack user

Chasing the dragon - crack and heroin

Chasing the tiger - to smoke heroin

Cheap basing - crack

Check - personal supply of drugs

Cheeba - marijuana

Cheeo - marijuana

Chemical - crack

Chewies - crack

Chiba chiba - high potency marijuana from Columbia

Chicago black - marijuana, term from Chicago

Chicago green - marijuana

Chicken powder - amphetamine

Chicken scratch - searching on hands and knees for crack

Chicle - heroin

Chief - LSD; mescaline

Chieva - heroin

China cat - high potency heroin

China girl - fentanyl

China town - fentanyl

China White - fentanyl

Chinese molasses - opium

Chinese red - heroin

Chinese tobacco - opium

Chip - heroin

Chipper - occasional Hispanic user

Chipping - using drugs occasionally

Chippy - cocaine

Chira - marijuana

Chiva - heroin

Chocolate - opium; amphetamine

Chocolate chips - LSD

Chocolate ecstasy - crack madebrown by adding chocolate
milk powder during production

Choe - cocaine

Cholly - cocaine

Chorals - depressant

Christina - amphetamine

Christmas rolls - depressant

Christmas tree - marijuana; depressant; amphetamine

Chronic - marijuana; marijuana mixed with crack

Chucks - hunger following withdrawal from heroin

Churus - marijuana

Chystal methadrine - amphetamine

Cid - LSD

Cigarette paper - packet of heroin

Cigarrode cristal - PCP

Citrol - high potency marijuana, from Nepal

CJ - PCP

Clarity - MDMA

Clear up - stop drug use

Clicker - crack and PCP

Cliffhanger - PCP

Climax - crack; isobutyl nitrite; heroin

Climb - marijuana cigarette

Clips - rows of vials heat-sealed together

Clocking paper - profits from selling drugs

Closet baser - user of crack who prefers anonymity

Cloud - crack

Cloud nine - crack

Cluck - crack smoker

Co-pilot - amphetamine

Coasting - under the influence of drugs

Coasts to coasts - amphetamine

Coca - cocaine

Cocaine blues - depression after extended cocaine use

Cochornis - marijuana

Cocktail - cigarette laced with cocaine or crack; smoked marijuana cigarette inserted in cigarette

Cocoa puff - to smoke cocaine and marijuana

Coconut - cocaine

Coco rocks - dark brown crack made by adding chocolate pudding during production

Coco snow - benzocaine used as cutting agent for crack

Cod - large amount of money

Coffee - LSD

Coke - cocaine; crack

Coke bar - bar where cocaine is openly used

Cola - cocaine

Cold turkey - sudden withdrawal from drugs

Coli - marijuana

Coliflor tostao - marijuana

Colorado cocktail - marijuana

Columbian - marijuana

Columbo - PCP

Columbus black - marijuana

Comeback - benzocaine and mannitol used to adulterate cocaine for conversion to crack

Come home - end a "trip" from LSD

Conductor - LSD

Connect - purchase drugs; supplier of illegal drugs

Contact lens - LSD

Cook - mix heroin with water; heating heroin to prepare it for injection

Cook down - process in which users liquify heroin in order to inhale it

Cooker to inject a drug

Cookies - crack

Coolie - cigarette laced with cocaine

Cooler - cigarette laced with a drug

Cop - obtain drugs

Copping zones - specific areas where buyers can purchase
drugs

Coral - depressant

Coriander seeds - cash

Corine - cocaine

Cork the air - to inhale cocaine

Corrinne - cocaine

Cosa - marijuana

Cotics - heroin

Coties - codeine

Cotton - currency

Cotton brothers - cocaine, heroin and morphine

Courage pills - heroin; depressant

Course note - bill larger than $2

Cozmo's - PCP

Crack - cocaine

Crack attack - craving for crack

Crack back - crack and marijuana

Crack cooler - crack soaked in wine cooler

Crack kits - glass pipe and copper mesh

Cracker jacks - crack smokers

Crackers - LSD

Crack gallery - place where crack is bought and sold

Crack spot - area where people can purchase crack

Crank - methamphetamine; amphetamine; methcathinone

Cranking up - to inject a drug

Crankster - person who uses or manufactures
methamphetamine

Crap/crop - low quality heroin

Crash - sleep off effects of drugs

Crazy coke - PCP

Crazy Eddie - PCP

Crazy weed - marijuana

Credit card - crack stem

Crib - crack

Crimmie - cigarette laced with crack

Crink - methamphetamine

Cripple - marijuana cigarette

Cris - methamphetamine

Crisscross - amphetamine

Criss-crossing - the practice of setting up a line of cocaine nect to a line of heroin. The user places a straw in each nostril and snorts about half a line each. Then the straws are crossed and the remaining lines are snorted.

Cristina - methamphetamine

Cristy - smokable methamphetamine

Croak - crack and methamphetamine

Cross tops - amphetamine

Crossroads - amphetamine

Crown crap - heroin

Crumbs - tiny pieces of crack

Crunch & Munch - crack

Cruz - opium from Veracruz, Mexico

Crying weed - marijuana

Crypto - methamphetamine

Crystal - methamphetamine; PCP; amphetamine; cocaine

Crystal joint - PCP

Crystal meth - methamphetamine

Cystal T - PCP

Crystal tea - LSD

Cube - 1 ounce; LSD

Cubes - marijuana tablets

Culican - high potency marijuana from Mexico

Cupcakes - LSD

Cura - heroin

Cushion - vein into which a drug is injected

Cut - adulterate drugs

Cut-deck - heroin mixed with powdered milk

Cycline - PCP

Cyclones - PCP

top

D - LSD, PCP

Dabble - use drugs occasionally

Dagga - marijuana

Dama blanca - cocaine

Dance fever - fentanyl

Dawamesk - marijuana

Dead on arrival - heroin

Debs - amphetamine

Decadence - MDMA

Deca-duabolin - injectable steroid

Deck - 1 to 15 grams of heroin, also known as a

bag; packet of drugs

Deeda - LSD

Delatestryl - injectable steroid

Demo - crack stem; a sample-size quantity of crack

Demolish - crack

Dep-testosterone - injectable steroid

DET - dimethyltryptamine

Detroit pink - PCP

Deuce - $2 worth of drugs; heroin

Devil's dandruff - crack

Devil's dick - crack pipe

Devil's dust - PCP

Devilsmoke - crack

Dew - marijuana

Dews - $10 worth of drugs

Dex - amphetamine

Dexedrine - amphetamine

Dexies - amphetamine

Diablito - combination of crack cocaine and marijuana in a joint

Diambista - marijuana

Diamonds - amphetamine

Dianabol - veterinary steroid

Dice - crack cocaine

Diesel - heroin

Diet pills - amphetamine

Dihydrolone - injectable steroid

Dimba - marijuana from West Africa

Dime - crack; $10 worth of crack

Dime bag - $10 worth of drugs

Dime special - crack cocaine

Dime's worth - amount of heroin to cause death

Ding - marijuana

Dinkie dow - marijuana

Dinosaurs - populations of heroin users in their forties or fifties

Dip - crack

Dipper - PCP

Dipping out - crack runners taking a portion of crack from vials

Dirt - heroin

Dirt grass - inferior quality marijuana

Dirty basing - crack

Dirty joints - combination of crack cocaine and marijuana

Disco biscuits - depressant

Disease - drug of choice

Ditch - marijuana

Ditch weed - marijuana inferior quality, Mexican

Djamba - marijuana

DMT - Dimethyltryptamine

Do a joint - to smoke marijuana

Do a line - to inhale cocaine

Do it Jack - PCP

DOA - PCP; crack

Doctor - MDMA

Dog - good friend

Dog food - heroin

Dogie - heroin

Dollar - $100 worth of drugs

Dolls - depressant

Domes - LSD

Domestic - locally grown marijuana

Domex - PCP and MDMA

Dominoes - amphetamine

Don jem - marijuana

Dona Juana - marijuana

Dona Juanita - marijuana

Doobee - marijuana

Doobie/dubbe/duby - marijuana

Doogie/doojee/dugie - heroin

Dooley - heroin

Dope - heroin; marijuana; any other drug

Dope fiend - crack addict

Dope smoke - to smoke marijuana

Dopium - opium

Doradilla - marijuana

Dors and 4's - combination of Doriden and Tyenol 4

Dots - LSD

Doub - $20 rock of crack

Double breasted dealing - dealing cocaine and heroin

together

Double bubble - cocaine

Double cross - amphetamine

Double dome - LSD

Double rock - crack diluted with procaine

Double trouble - depressant

Double up - when a crack dealerdelivers an extra rock

as a marketing ploy to attract customers

Double ups - a $20 rock that can be broken into two $20

rocks

Double yoke - crack

Dove - $35 piece of crack

Dover's powder - opium

Downer - depressant

Downie - depressant

Draf weed - marijuana

Drag weed - marijuana

Draw up - to inject a drug

Dream - cocaine

Dream gum - opium

Dream stick - opium

Dreamer - morphine

Dreams - opium

Dreck - heroin

Drink - PCP

Drivers - amphetamine

Dropper - to inject a drug

Drowsy high - depressant

Dry high - marijuana

Dub - when a crack dealer delivers an extra rock

as a marketing ploy to attract customers

Dube - marijuana

Duby - marijuana

Duct - cocaine

'Due - residue of oils trapped in a pipe after

smoking base

Duji - heroin

Dummy dust - PCP

Durabolin - injectable steroid

Durog - marijuana

Duros - marijuana

Dust - heroin; cocaine; PCP; marijuana mixed with

various chemicals

Dust joint - PCP

Dust of angels - PCP

Dusted parsley - PCP

Dusting - adding PCP, heroin, or another drug to marijuana

Dymethzine - injectable steroid

Dynamite - heroin and cocaine

Dyno - heroin

Dyno-pure - heroin

Earth - marijuana cigarette

Easing powder - opium

Eastside player - crack

Easy score - obtaining drugs easily

Eating - taking a drug orally

Ecstasy - MDMA

Egg - crack

Eight ball - 1/8 ounce of drugs

Eightball - crack and heroin

Eighth - heroin

El diablito - marijuana, cocaine, heroin and PCP

El diablo - marijuana, cocaine and heroin

Electric Kool Aid - LSD

Elephant - PCP

Elephant tranquilizer - PCP

Elvis - LSD

Embalming fluid - PCP

Emergency gun - instrument used to inject other than

syringe

Emsel - morphine

Endo - marijuana

Energizer - PCP

Enoltestovis - injectable steroid

Ephedrone - methcathinone

Equipose - veterinary steroid

Erth - PCP

Esra - marijuana

Essence - MDMA

Estuffa - heroin

ET - alpha-ethyltyptamine

Eve - MDEA

Explorers club - group of LSD users

Eye opener - crack; amphetamine

Factory - place where drugs are packaged, diluted,

or

manufactured

Fake STP - PCP

Fall - arrested

Fallbrook redhair - marijuana, term from Fallbrook, CA

Famous dimes - crack

Fastin - amphetamine

Fantasia - dimethyltryptamine

Fat bags - crack

Fatty - marijuana cigarette

Feed bag - container for marijuana

Felix the Cat - LSD

Ferry dust - heroin

Fi-do-nie - opium

Fields - LSD

Fiend - someone who smokes marijuana alone

Fifteen cents - $15 worth of drugs

Fifty-one - crack

Finajet/finaject - veterinary steroid

Fine stuff - marijuana

Finger - marijuana cigarette

Finger lid - marijuana

Fir - marijuana

Fire - to inject a drug; crack and
methamphetamine

Fire it up - to smoke marijuana

First line - morphine

Fish scales - crack

Five cent bag - $5 worth of drugs

Five C note - $500 bill

Five dollar bag - $50 worth of drugs

Fives - amphetamine

Fix - to inject a drug

Fizzies - methadone

Flag - appearance of blood in the vein

Flake - cocaine

Flakes - PCP

Flame cooking - smoking cocaine base by putting the pipe over a stove flame

Flamethrowers - cigarette laced with cocaine and heroin

Flash - LSD

Flat blues - LSD

Flat chunks - crack cut with benzocaine

Flea powder - low purity heroin

Florida snow - cocaine

Flower - marijuana

Flower tops - marijuana

Fly Mexican airlines - to smoke marijuana

Flying - under the influence of drugs

Following that cloud - searching for drugs

Foo foo stuff - heroin; cocaine

Foo-foo dust - cocaine

Foolish powder - heroin; cocaine

Footballs - amphetamine

Forget pill - Rohypnol

Forget me drug - Rohypnol

45 Minute Psychosis - Dimethyltryptamine

Forwards - amphetamine

Fraho/frajo - marijuana

Freebase - smoking cocaine; crack

Freeze - cocaine; renege on a drug deal

French blue - amphetamine

French fries - crack

Fresh - PCP

Friend - fentanyl

Fries - crack

Frios - marijuana laced with PCP

Frisco special - cocaine, heroin and LSD

Frisco speedball - cocaine, heroin and LSD

Friskie powder - cocaine

Fry - crack

Fry daddy - crack and marijuana; cigarette laced with crack

Fu - marijuana

Fuel - marijuana mixed with insecticides; PCP

Fuete - hypodermic needle

Fuma D'Angola - marijuana Portugese term

top

G - $1000 or 1 gram of drugs; term for an unfamiliar male

G.B. - depressant

GHB - gamma hydroxy butyrate

G-rock - one gram of rock cocaine

G-shot - small dose of drugs used to hold off withdrawal symptoms until full dose can be taken

Gaffel - fake cocaine

Gaffus - hypodermic needle

Gage/gauge - marijuana

Gagers - methcathinone

Gaggers - methcathinone

Galloping horse - heroin

Gamot - heroin

Gange - marijuana

Gangster - marijuana

Gangster pills - depressant

Ganja - marijuana from Jamaica

Gank - fake crack

Garbage - inferior quality drugs

Garbage heads - users who buy crack from street dealers instead of cooking it themselves

Garbage rock - crack

Gash - marijuana

Gasper - marijuana cigarette

Gasper stick - marijuana cigarette

Gato - heroin

Gauge butt - marijuana

Gee - opium

Geek - crack and marijuana

Geek joints - cigarettes or cigars filled with tobacco and crack

Geeker - crack user

Geeze - to inhale cocaine

Geezer - to inject a drug

Geezin a bit of dee gee - injecting a drug

Georgia home boy - gamma hydroxy butyrate

George smack - heroin

Get a gage up - to smoke marijuana

Get a gift - obtain drugs

Get down - to inject a drug

Get high - to smoke marijuana

Get lifted - under the influence of drugs

Get off - to inject a drug; get "high"

Get off houses - private places heroin users can purchase

& use heroin for a fee

Get the wind - to smoke marijuana

Get through - obtain drugs

Getting roached - using Rohypnol

Ghana - marijuana

Ghost - LSD

Ghost busting - smoking cocaine; searching for white

particles in the belief that they are

crack

Gick monster - crack smoker

Gift-of-the-sun - cocaine

Giggle smoke - marijuana

Giggle weed - marijuana

Gimmick - drug injection equipment

Gimmie - crack and marijuana

Gin - cocaine

Girl - cocaine; crack; heroin

Girlfriend - cocaine

Giro houses - non-bank financial institutions frequently

usedby drug traffickers to launder drug

proceeds

Give wings - inject someone or teach someone to inject

heroin

Glacines - heroin

Glad stuff - cocaine

Glading - using inhalant

Glass - hypodermic needle; amphetamine

Glass gun - hypodermic needle

Glo - crack

Gluey - person who sniffs glue

Go - amphetamines

Go-fast - methcathinone

Go into a sewer - to inject a drug

Go loco - to smoke marijuana

Go on a sleigh ride - to inhale cocaine

Goblet of jam - marijuana

God's flesh - psilocybin/psilocin

God's medicine - opium

God's drug - morphine

Gold - marijuana; crack

Gold dust - cocaine

Gold star - marijuana

Golden - marijuana

Golden Dragon - LSD

Golden girl - heroin

Golden leaf - very high quality marijuana

Golf ball - crack

Golf balls - depressant

Golpe - heroin

Goma - opium; black tar heroin

Gondola - opium

Gong - marijuana; opium

Gonj - marijuana

Goob - methcathinone

Good - PCP

Good and plenty - heroin

Good butt - marijuana cigarette

Good giggles - marijuana

Good go - proper amount of drugs for the money paid

Good H - heroin

Good lick - good drugs

Goodfellas - fentanyl

Goody-goody - marijuana

Goof butt - marijuana cigarette

Goofball - cocaine and heroin; depressant

Goofers - depressant

Goofy's - LSD

Goon - PCP

Goon dust - PCP

Gopher - person paid to pickup drugs

Goric - opium

Gorilla tab - PCP

Gorilla biscuits - PCP

Gorilla pills - depressant

Got it going on - fast sale of drugs

Graduate - completely stop using drugs or progress to

stronger drugs

Gram - hashish

Grape parfait - LSD

Grass - marijuana

Grass brownies - marijuana

Grasshopper - marijuana

Grata - marijuana

Gravel - crack

Gravy - to inject a drug; heroin

Grease - currency

Great bear - fentanyl

Great tobacco - opium

Green - inferior quality marijuana; PCP; ketamine

Green buds - marijuana

Green double domes - LSD

Green dragons - depressant

Green frog - depressant

Green goddess - marijuana

Green gold - cocaine

Green goods - paper currency

Green leaves - PCP

Green single domes - LSD

Green tea - PCP

Green wedge - LSD

Greens/green stuff - paper currency

Greenies - amphetamine

Greeter - marijuana

Greta - marijuana

Grey shields - LSD

Griefo - marijuana

Griefs - marijuana

Grievous bodily harm - GHB

Grifa - marijuana

Griff - marijuana

Griffa - marijuana

Griffo - marijuana

Grit - crack

Groceries - crack

Ground control - guide or caretaker during a hallucinogenic experience

Gum - opium

Guma - opium

Gun - to inject a drug; needle

Gunga - marijuana

Gungeon - marijuana

Gungun - marijuana

Gunja - marijuana

Gutter - vein into which a drug is injected

Gutter junkie - addict who relies on others to obtain drugs

Gyve - marijuana cigarette

top

H - heroin

H & C - heroin and cocaine

H Caps - heroin

Hache - heroin

Hail - crack

Haircut - marijuana

Hairy - heroin

Half - 1/2 ounce

Half-a-C - $50 bill

Half a football field - 50 rocks of crack

Half G - $500

Half load - 15 bags (decks) of heroin

Half moon - peyote

Half piece - 1/2 ounce of heroin or cocaine

Half track - crack

Hamburger helper - crack

Hand-to-hand - direct delivery and payment

Hand-to-hand man - transient dealers who carry small

amounts

of crack

Hanhich - marijuana

Hanyak - smokable speed

Happy cigarette - marijuana cigarette

Happy dust - cocaine

Happy powder - cocaine

Happy sticks - PCP

Happy trails - cocaine

Hard candy - heroin

Hard line - crack

Hard rock - crack

Hard stuff - opium; heroin

Hardware - isobutyl nitrite

Harry - heroin

Harsh - marijuana

Hats - LSD

Has - marijuana

Have a dust - cocaine

Haven dust - cocaine

Hawaiin - very high potency marijuana

Hawaiian sunshine - LSD

Hawk - LSD

Hay - marijuana

Hay butt - marijuana cigarette

Haze - LSD

Hazel - heroin

HCP - PCP

Head drugs - amphetamine

Headlights - LSD

Heart-on - inhalant

Hearts - amphetamine

Heaven and Hell - PCP

Heaven dust - heroin; cocaine

Heavenly blue - LSD

Heeled - having plenty of money

Helen - heroin

Hell dust - heroin

He-man - fentanyl

Hemp - marijuana

Henpicking - searching on hands and knees for crack

Henry - heroin

Henry VIII - cocaine

Her - cocaine

Herb - marijuana

Herb and Al - marijuana and alcohol

Herba - marijuana

Herms - PCP

Hero - heroin

Hero of the underworld - heroin

Heroina - heroin

Herone - heroin

Hessle - heroin

Highbeams - the wide eyes of a person on crack

Hikori - peyote

Hikuli - peyote

Him - heroin

Hinkley - PCP

Hippie crack - inhalant

Hiropon - smokable methamphetamine

Hit - crack; marijuana cigarette; to smoke

marijuana

Hit the hay - to smoke marijuana

Hit the house - house where users go to shoot up and leave
the the owner drugs as payment

Hit the main line - to inject a drug

Hit the needle - to inject a drug

Hit the pit - to inject a drug

Hitch up the reindeers - to inhale cocaine

Hitter - little pipe designed for only one hit

Hitting up - injecting drugs

Hocus - opium; marijuana

Hog - PCP

Holding - possessing drugs

Hombre - heroin

Hombrecitos - psilocybin

Homegrown - marijuana

Honey - currency

Honey blunts - Marijuana cigars sealed with honey

Honey oil - ketamine; inhalant

Honeymoon - early stages of drug use before addiction
or dependency develops

Hong-yen - heroin in pill form

Hooch - marijuana

Hooked - addicted

Hooter - cocaine; marijuana

Hop/hops - opium

Hopped up - under the influence of drugs

Horn - to inhale cocaine; crack pipe

Horning - heroin; to inhale cocaine

Horse - heroin

Horse heads - amphetamine

Horse tracks - PCP

Horse tranquilizer - PCP

Hot dope - heroin

Hot heroin - poisoned to give to a police informant

Hot ice - smokable methamphetamine

Hot load/hot shot - lethal injection of an opiate

Hot rolling - liquefying methamphetamine in an eye dropper and then inhaling it

Hot stick - marijuana cigarette

Hotcakes - crack

House fee - money paid to enter a crackhouse

House piece - crack given to the owner of a crackhouse or apartment where crack users congregate

How do you like me now? - crack

Hows - morphine

HRN - heroin

Hubba - crack

Hubba, I am back - crack

Hubba pigeon - crack user looking for rocks on a floor after a police raid

Hubbas - crack, term from Northern CA

Huff - inhalant

Huffer - inhalant abuser

Hulling - using others to get drugs

Hunter - cocaine

Hustle - attempt to obtain drug customers

Hyatari - peyote

Hydro - amphetamine

Hype - heroin addict; an addict

Hype stick - hypodermic needle

top

I am back - crack

Iboga - amphetamine

Ice - cocaine; methamphetamine; smokeable

amphetamine; MDMA, PCP

Ice cream habit - occasional use of drugs

Ice cube - crack

Icing - cocaine

Idiot pills - depressant

Ill - PCP

Illies - beedies dipped in PCP

Illy momo - PCP

In - connected with drug suppliers

Inbetweens - depressant; amphetamine

Inca message - cocaine

Indian boy - marijuana

Indian hay - marijuana from India

Indica - species of cannabis, found in hot climate,

grows 3.5 to 4 feet

Indian hemp - marijuana

Indica - species of cannabis, found in hot climate,

grows 3.5 to 4 feet

Indo - marijuana, term from Northern CA

Indonesian bud - marijuana; opium

Instaga - marijuana

Instagu - marijuana

Instant zen - LSD

Interplanetary mission - travel from one crackhouse to

another in

search of crack

Isda - heroin

Issues - crack

J - marijuana cigarette

Jab/job - to inject a drug

Jack - steal someone else's drugs

Jackpot - fentanyl

Jack-Up - to inject a drug

Jag - keep a high going

Jam - amphetamine; cocaine

Jam cecil - amphetamine

Jamaican gold - marijuana

Jane - marijuana

Jay smoke - marijuana

Jay - marijuana cigarette

Jee gee - heroin

Jefferson airplane - used match cut in half to hold a
partially
smoked marijuana cigarette

Jellies - depressant

Jelly - cocaine

Jelly baby - amphetamine

Jelly bean - amphetamine; depressant

Jelly beans - crack

Jet - ketamine

Jet fuel - PCP

Jim Jones - marijuana laced with cocaine and PCP

Jive - heroin; marijuana; drugs

Jive doo jee - heroin

Jive stick - marijuana

Johnson - crack

Joint - marijuana cigarette

Jojee - heroin

Jolly bean - amphetamine

Jolly green - marijuana

Jolly pop - casual user of heroin

Jolt - to inject a drug; strong reaction to drugs

Jones - heroin

Jonesing - need for drugs

Joy flakes - heroin

Joy juice - depressant

Joy plant - opium

Joy pop - to inject a drug

Joy popping - occasional use of drugs

Joy powder - heroin; cocaine

Joy smoke - marijuana

Joy stick - marijuana cigarette

Ju-ju - marijuana cigarette

Juan Valdez - marijuana

Juanita - marijuana

Juggle - sell drugs to another addict to support a
habit

Juggler - teen-aged street dealer

Jugs - amphetamine

Juice - steroids, PCP

Juice joint - marijuana cigarette sprinkled with crack

Juja - marijuana

Jum - sealed plastic bag containing crack

Jumbos - large vials of crack sold on the streets

Junk - cocaine; heroin

Junkie - addict

Junkie kits - glass pipe and copper mesh

top

K - PCP

Kabayo - heroin

Kabuki - crack pipe made from a plastic rum bottle
and a rubber sparkplug cover

Kaksonjae - smokable methamphetamine

Kali - marijuana

Kansas grass - marijuana

Kangaroo - crack

Kaps - PCP

Karachi - heroin

Kate bush - marijuana

Kaya - marijuana

K-blast - PCP

Kee - marijuana

Kentucky blue - marijuana

Key - marijuana

KGB (killer green bud) - marijuana

K-hole - periods of ketamine-induced confusion

Khat - amphetamine; methcathinone

Ki - marijuana

Kibbles & Bits - small crumbs of crack

Kick - getting off a drug habit; inhalant

Kick stick - marijuana cigarette

Kiddie dope - prescription drugs

Kiff - marijuana

Killer - marijuana; PCP

Killer green bud - marijuana

Killer joints - PCP

Killer weed (1980s) - marijuana and PCP

Killer weed (1960s) - marijuana

Kilo - 2.2 pounds

Kilter - marijuana

Kind - marijuana

King bud - marijuana

King ivory - fentanyl

King Kong pills - depressant

King's habit - cocaine

Kissing - the exchange of plastic wrapped rocks (crack) by

kissing or mouth to mouth transfer

Kit - equipment used to inject drugs

KJ - PCP

Kleenex - MDMA

Klingons - crack addicts

Kokomo - crack

Koller joints - PCP

Kools - PCP

Kryptonite - crack

Krystal - PCP

Krystal joint - PCP

Kumba - marijuana

KW - PCP

L - LSD

L.A. - long-acting amphetamine

L.A. glass - smokable methamphetamine

L.A. ice - smokable methamphetamine

L.L. - marijuana

Lace - cocaine and marijuana

Lady - cocaine

Lady caine - cocaine

Lady snow - cocaine

Lakbay diva - marijuana

Lamborghini - crack pipe made from plastic rum bottle
and a rubber sparkplug cover

Las mujercitas - psilocybin

Lason sa daga - LSD

Late night - cocaine

Laugh and scratch - to inject a drug

Laughing gas - nitrous oxide

Laughing grass - marijuana

Laughing weed - marijuana

Lay back - depressant

Lay-out - equipment for taking drugs

LBJ - LSD; PCP; heroin

Leaky bolla - PCP

Leaky leak - PCP

Leaf - marijuana; cocaine

Leapers - amphetamine

Leaping - under the influence of drugs

Legal speed - over the counter asthma drug; trate name

= Mini thin

Lemon 714 - PCP

Lemon drop - methamphetamine with a dull yellow tint

Lemonade - heroin; poor quality drugs

Lenos - PCP

Lens - LSD

Lethal weapon - PCP

Lettuce - money

Lib (Librium) - depressant

Lid - 1 ounce of marijuana

Lid proppers - amphetamine

Light stuff - marijuana

Lightning - amphetamine

Lima - marijuana

Lime acid - LSD

Line - cocaine

Lipton Tea - inferior quality drugs

Liquid ecstasty - GHB

Lit up - under the influence of drugs

Little bomb - amphetamine; heroin; depressant

Little ones - PCP

Little smoke - marijuana; psilocybin/psilocin

Live ones - PCP

Llesca - marijuana

Load - 25 bags of heroin

Loaded - high

Loaf - marijuana

Lobo - marijuana

Locker room - isobutyl nitrite

Loco - marijuana

Locoweed - marijuana

Log - PCP; marijuana cigarette

Logor - LSD

Loony toons - LSD

Loused - covered by sores and abscesses from

repeated use of unsterile needles

Love - crack

Love affair - cocaine

Love boat - marijuana dipped in formaldehyde; PCP;

blunts mixed with marijuana

and heroin

Love drug - MDMA; depressant

Love pearls - alpha-ethyltyptamine

Love pills - alpha-ethyltyptamine

Love trip - MDMA and mescaline

Love weed - marijuana

Lovelies - marijuana laced with PCP

Lovely - PCP

LSD - lysergic acid diethylamide

Lubage - marijuana

Lucy in the sky with diamonds - LSD

Ludes - depressant

Luding out - depressant

Luds - depressant

Lunch money drugs - rohypnol

top

M - marijuana; morphine

M.J. - marijuana

M.O. - marijuana

M.S. - morphine

M.U. - marijuana

M&M - depressant

Machinery - marijuana

Macon - marijuana

Maconha - marijuana

Madman - PCP

Mad dog - PCP

Magic - PCP

Magic dust - PCP

Magic mushroom - psilocybin/psilocin

Magic smoke - marijuana

Main line - to inject a drug

Mainliner - person who injects into the vein

Make up - need to find more drugs

Mama coca - cocaine

Manhattan silver - marijuana

MAO - amphetamine

Marathons - amphetamine

Mari - marijuana cigarette

Marshmallow reds - depressant

Mary - marijuana

Mary and Johnny - marijuana

Mary Ann - marijuana

Mary Jane - marijuana

Mary Jonas - marijuana

Mary Warner - marijuana

Mary Weaver - marijuana

Maserati - crack pipe made from a plastic rum bottle

and rubber sparkplug cover

Matchbox - 1/4 ounce of marijuana or 6 marijuana

cigarettes

Matsakow - heroin

Maui wauie - marijuana from Hawaii

Max - gamma hydroxy butyrate dissolved in water

and

mixed with amphetamines

Maxibolin - oral steroid

Mayo - cocaine; heroin

MDM - MDMA

MDMA - methylenedioxy-methamphetamine

Mean green - PCP

Medusa - inhalant

Meg - marijuana

Megg - marijuana cigarette

Meggie - marijuana

Mellow yellow - LSD

Merchandise - drugs

Merck - cocaine

Merk - cocaine

Mesc - mescaline

Mescal - mescaline

Mese - mescaline

Messorole - marijuana

Meth - methamphetamine

Meth head - regular user of methamphetamine

Meth monster - person who has a violent reaction to
methamphetamine

Meth speed ball - methamphetamine combined with heroin

Methatriol - injectable steroid

Methedrine - amphetamine

Methlies Quik - amphetamines

Methyltestosterone - oral steroid

Mexican brown - heroin; marijuana

Mexican crack - methamphetamine with the appearance of crack

Mexican green - marijuana

Mexican horse - heroin

Mexican locoweed - marijuana

Mexican mud - heroin

Mexican mushroom - psilocybin/psilocin

Mexican red - marijuana

Mexican reds - depressant

Mexican valiums - rohypnol

Mezc - mescaline

Mickey Finn - depressant

Mickey's - depressant

Microdot - LSD

Midnight oil - opium

Mighty Quinn - LSD

Mighty Joe Young - depressant

Mighty mezz - marijuana cigarette

Mind detergent - LSD

Mini beans - amphetamine

Minibennie - amphetamine

Mint leaf - PCP

Mint weed - PCP

Mira - opium

Miss - to inject a drug

Miss Emma - morphine

Missile basing - crack liquid and PCP

Mission - trip out of the crackhouse to obtain crack

Mist - PCP; crack smoke

Mister blue - morphine

Mixed jive - crack cocaine

Modams - marijuana

Mohasky - marijuana

Mojo - cocaine; heroin

Monkey - drug dependency; cigarette made from

cocaine

paste and tobacco

Monkey dust - PCP

Monkey tranquilizer - PCP

Monoamine oxidase - amphetamine

Monos - cigarette made from cocaine paste and

tobacco

Monte - marijuana from South America

Mooca/moocah - marijuana

Moon - mescaline

Moon gas - inhalant

Moonrock - crack and heroin

Mooster - marijuana

Moota/mutah - marijuana

Mooters - marijuana cigarette

Mootie - marijuana

Mootos - marijuana

Mor a grifa - marijuana

More - PCP

Morf - morphine

Morning shoot - amphetamine

Morning wake-up - first blast of crack from the pipe

Morotgara - heroin

Morpho - morphine

Mortal combat - high potency heroin

Mosquitos - cocaine

Mota/moto - marijuana

Mother - marijuana

Mother's little helper - depressant

Mouth worker - one who takes drugs orally

Movie star drug - cocaine

Mow the grass - to smoke marijuana

Mu - marijuana

Mud - opium; heroin

Muggie - marijuana

Muggles - marijuana

Mujer - cocaine

Mule - carrier of drugs

Murder one - heroin and cocaine

Murder 8 - fentanyl

Mushrooms - psilocybin/psilocin

Musk - psilocybin/psilocin

Muta - marijuana

Mutha - marijuana

Muzzle - heroin

top

Nail - marijuana cigarette

Nailed - arrested

Nanoo - heroin

Nebbies - depressant

Nemmies - depressant

New acid - PCP

New addition - crack cocaine

New magic - PCP

New Jack Swing - heroin and morphine

Nexus - 2C-B

Nice and easy - heroin

Nickel bag - $5 worth of drugs; heroin

Nickel deck - heroin

Nickel note - $5 bill

Nickelonians - crack addicts

Niebla - PCP

Nigra - marijuana

Nimbies - depressant

Nineteen - amphetamine

Nix - stranger among the group

Nod - effects of heroin

Noise - heroin

Nontoucher - crack user who doesn't want affection during or after smoking crack

Nose - heroin

Nose candy - cocaine

Nose drops - liquified heroin

Nose stuff - cocaine

Nose powder - cocaine

Nubs - peyote

Nugget - amphetamine

Nuggets - crack

Number - marijuana cigarette

Number 3 - cocaine, heroin

Number 4 - heroin

Number 8 - heroin

O - opium

O.J. - marijuana

O.P. - opium

O.P.P. - PCP

Octane - PCP laced with gasoline

Ogoy - heroin

Oil - heroin, PCP

Old Steve - heroin

On a mission - searching for crack

On a trip - under the influence of drugs

On ice - in jail

On the bricks - walking the streets

On the nod - under the influence of narcotics or

depressant

One and one - to inhale cocaine

One box tissue - one ounce of crack

One on one house - where cocaine and heroin can be

purchased

One-fifty-one - crack

One plus one sales - selling cocaine and heroin together

One way - LSD

Oolies - marijuana cigarettes laced with crack

Ope - opium

Optical illusions - LSD

Orange barrels - LSD

Orange crystal - PCP

Orange cubes - LSD

Orange haze - LSD

Orange micro - LSD

Orange wedges - LSD

Oranges - amphetamine

Outerlimits - crack and LSD

Owsley - LSD

Owsley's acid - LSD

Oyster stew - cocaine

Oz - inhalant

Ozone - PCP

top

P - peyote, PCP

PCP - phencyclidine

PCPA - PCP

P.R. (Panama Red) - marijuana

P-dope - 20-30% pure heroin

P-funk - heroin; crack and PCP

Pack - heroin; marijuana

Pack a bowl - marijuana

Pack of rocks - marijuana cigarette

Pakalolo - marijuana

Pakistani black - marijuana

Panama cut - marijuana

Panama gold - marijuana

Panama red - marijuana

Panatella - large marijuana cigarette

Panckes and syrup - Combination of glutethimide and

codeine

cough syrup

Pane - LSD

Pangonadalot - heroin

Panic - drugs not available

Paper - a dosage unit of heroin

Paper acid - LSD

Paper bag - container for drugs

Paper blunts - marijuana within a paper casing rather

than a tobacco leaf casing

Paper boy - heroin peddler

Parabolin - veterinary steroid

Parachute - crack and PCP smoked; heroin

Paradise - cocaine

Paradise white - cocaine

Parlay - crack

Parsley - marijuana, PCP

Paste - crack

Pat - marijuana

Patico - crack (Spanish)

Paz - PCP

Peace - LSD, PCP

Peace pill - PCP

Peace tablets - LSD

Peace weed - PCP

Peaches - amphetamine

Peanut - depressant

Peanut butter - PCP mixed with peanut butter

Pearl - cocaine

Pearls - amyl nitrite

Pearly gates - LSD

Pebbles - crack

Peddlar - drug supplier

Pee Wee - crack; $5 worth of crack

Peep - PCP

Peg - heroin

Pellets - LSD

Pen yan - opium

Pep pills - amphetamine

Pepsi habit - occasional use of drugs

Perfect High - heroin

Perico - cocaine

Perlas - street dealer (heroin)

Perp - fake crack made of candle wax and baking soda

Peter Pan - PCP

Peth - depressant

Peruvian - cocaine

Peruvian flake - cocaine

Peruvian lady - cocaine

Peyote - mescaline

Phennies - depressant

Phenos - depressant

Pianoing - using the fingers to find lost crack

Piece - 1 ounce; cocaine; crack

Piedras - crack (Spanish)

Pig Killer - PCP

Piles - crack

Pimp - cocaine

Pimp your pipe - lending or renting your crack pipe

Pin - marijuana

Pin gon - opium

Pin yen - opium

Ping-in-wing - to inject a drug

Pingus - rohypnol

Pink blotters - LSD

Pink hearts - amphetamine

Pink ladies - depressant

Pink Panther - LSD

Pink robots - LSD

Pink wedge - LSD

Pink witches - LSD

Pipe - crack pipe; marijuana pipe; vein into
which a drug is injected; mix drugs with
other substances

Pipero - crack user

Pit - PCP

Pixies - amphetamine

Plant - hiding place for drugs

Pocket rocket - marijuana

Pod - marijuana

Poison - heroin; fentanyl

Point - a needle

Poke - marijuana

Pole - mixture of heroin and motion sickness drug

Pollutants - amphetamine

Polvo - heroin; PCP

Polvo blanco - cocaine

Polvo de angel - PCP

Polvo de estrellas - PCP

Pony - crack

Poor man's pot - inhalant

Pop - to inhale cocaine

Poppers - isobutyl nitrite; amyl nitrite

Poppy - heroin

Pot - marijuana

Potato - LSD

Potato chips - crack cut with benzocaine

Potlikker - marijuana

Potten bush - marijuana

Powder - heroin; amphetamine

Powder diamonds - cocaine

Power puller - rubber piece attached to crack stem

Pox - opium

Predator - heroin

Prescription - marijuana cigarette

Press - cocaine; crack

Pretendica - marijuana

Pretendo - marijuana

Primo - crack; marijuana mixed with crack

Primobolan - injectable and oral steroid

Primos - cigarettes laced with cocaine and heroin

Proviron - oral steroid

Pseudocaine - phenylpropanolamine, an adulterant for

cutting crack

Puff the dragon - to smoke marijuana

Puffer - crack smoker

Puffy - PCP

Pulborn - heroin

Pullers - crack users who pull at parts of their

bodies excessively

Pumping - selling crack

Pure - heroin

Pure love - LSD

Purple - ketamine

Purple barrels - LSD

Purple haze - LSD

Purple hearts - LSD; amphetamine; depressant

Purple flats - LSD

Purple ozoline - LSD

Purple rain - PCP

Push - sell drugs

Push shorts - to cheat or sell short amounts

Pusher - one who sells drugs; metal hanger or

umbrella - rod used to scrape residue in crack stems

top

Q - depressant

Qat - methcathinone

Quad - depressant

Quarter - 1/4 ounce or $25 worth of drugs

Quarter bag - $25 worth of drugs

Quarter moon - hashish

Quarter piece - 1/4 ounce

Quartz - smokable speed

Quas - depressant

Queen Ann's lace - marijuana

Quicksilver - isobutyl nitrite

Quill - methamphetamine; heroin; cocaine

Quinolone - injectable steroid

R2 - Rohypnol

Racehorse charlie - cocaine; heroin

Ragweed - inferior quality marijuana; heroin

Railroad weed - marijuana

Rainbow - LSD

Rainbows - depressant

Rainy day woman - marijuana

Rambo - heroin

Rane - cocaine; heroin

Rangood - marijuana grown wild

Rap - criminally charged; to talk with someone

Raspberry - female who trades sex for crack or money
to buy crack

Rasta weed - marijuana

Raw - crack

Raw fusion - heroin

Raw hide - heroin

Rave - party designed to enhance a hallucinogenic
experience through music and behavior

Razed - under the influence of drugs

Ready rock - cocaine; crack; heroin

Recompress - change the shape of cocaine flakes to
resemble "rock"

Recycle - LSD

Red - under the influence of drugs

Red and blue - depressant

Red bullets - depressant

Red bud - marijuana

Red caps - crack

Red cross - marijuana

Red chicken - heroin

Red devil - depressant, PCP

Red dirt - marijuana

Reds - depressant

Red eagle - heroin

Red lips - LSD

Red phosphorus - smokable speed

Redneck cocaine - methamphetamine

Reefer - marijuana

Regular P - crack

Reindeer dust - heroin

Rest in peace - crack cocaine

Reynolds - rohypnol

Rhine - heroin

Rhythm - amphetamine

Rib - rohypnol

Riding the wave - under the influence of drugs

Rig - equipment used to inject drugs

Righteous bush - marijuana

Ringer - good hit of crack

Rip - marijuana

Rippers - amphetamine

Roach - butt of marijuana cigarette

Roach clip - holds partially smoked marijuana cigarette

Roaches - rohypnol

Road dope - amphetamine

Roapies - rohypnol

Roasting - smoking marijuana

Robutal - rohypnol

Roca - crack (Spanish)

Rochas dos - rohypnol

Roche - Rophynol; (see "roofies")

Rock attack - crack

Rock house - place where crack is sold and smoked

Rock(s) - cocaine; crack

Rocket caps - dome-shaped caps on crack vials

Rocket fuel - PCP

Rockets - marijuana cigarette

Rockette - female who uses crack

Rocks of hell - crack

Rock star - female who trades sex for crack or money to buy crack

Rocky III - crack

Roid rage - aggressive behavior caused by excessive steroid use

Roller - to inject a drug

Rollers - police

Rolling - MDMA

Roofies - Rophynol; a sedative that makes users feel very drunk

Rooster - crack

Root - marijuana

Rope - marijuana

Rophies - rohypnol

Rophy - rohypnol

Roples - rophynol

Rosa - amphetamine

Rose marie - marijuana

Roses - amphetamine

Rough stuff - marijuana

Rox - crack

Roxanne - cocaine; crack

Row-shay - rohypnol

Royal blues - LSD

Roz - crack

Ruderalis - species of cannabis, found in Russia,

grows 1 to 2.5 feet

Ruffies - Rophynol

Ruffles - Rophynol

Runners - people who sell drugs for others

Running - MDMA

Rush - isobutyl nitrite

Rush snappers - isobutyl nitrite

Russian sickles - LSD

top

Sack - heroin

Sacrament - LSD

Sacre mushroom - psilocybin

Salt - heroin

Salt and pepper - marijuana

Sam - federal narcotics agent

Sancocho - to steal (Spanish)

Sandoz - LSD

Sandwich - two layers of cocaine with a layer of

heroin in the middle

Santa Marta - marijuana

Sasfras - marijuana

Satan's secret - inhalant

Satch - papers, letter, cards, clothing, etc.,

saturated with drug solution (used to

smuggle drugs into prisons or hospitals)

Satch cotton - fabric used to filter a solution of

narcotics before injection

Sativa - species of cannabis, found in cool, damp

climate, grows up to 18 feet

Scaffle - PCP

Scag - heroin

Scat - heroin

Scate - heroin

Schmeck - cocaine

Schoolboy - cocaine, codeine

Schoolcraft - crack

Scissors - marijuana

Scooby snacks - MDMA

Scoop - GHB

Score - purchase drugs

Scorpion - cocaine

Scott - heroin

Scottie - cocaine

Scotty - cocaine; crack; the high from crack

Scramble - crack

Scrape and snort - to share crack by scraping off small pieces for snorting

Scratch - money

Scruples - crack

Scuffle - PCP

Seccy - depressant

Second to none - heroin

Seeds - marijuana

Seggy - depressant

Sen - marijuana

Seni - peyote

Serial speedballing - sequencing cocaine, cough syrup, and heroin over a 1-2 day period

Sernyl - PCP

Serpico 21 - cocaine

Server - crack dealer

Sess - marijuana

Set - place where drugs are sold

Sevenup - cocaine; crack

Sewer - vein into which a drug is injected

Sezz - marijuana

Shabu - ice

Shake - marijuana

Shaker/baker/water - materials needed to freebase cocaine; shaker bottle, baking soda, water

Sharps - needles

She - cocaine

Sheets - PCP

Sheet rocking - crack and LSD

Shermans - PCP

Sherm sticks - PCP

Sherms - PCP; crack

Sh*t - heroin

Shmeck/schmeek - heroin

Shoot - heroin

Shoot/shoot up - to inject a drug

Shoot the breeze - nitrous oxide

Shooting gallery - place where drugs are used

Shot - to inject a drug

Shot down - under the influence of drugs

Shrooms - psilocybin/psilocin

Siddi - marijuana

Sightball - crack

Silly Putty   psilocybin/psilocin

Simple Simon - psilocybin/ psilocin

Sinse - marijuana

Sinsemilla - potent variety marijuana

Sixty-two - 2 1/2 ounces of crack

Skee - opium

Skeegers/skeezers - crack-smoking prostitute

Sketching - coming down from a speed induced high

Skid - heroin

Skied - under the influence of drugs

Skin popping - injecting drugs under the skin

Skuffle - PCP

Skunk - marijuana

Slab - crack

Slam - to inject a drug

Slammin'/Slamming - amphetamine

Slanging - selling drugs

Sleeper - heroin; depressant

Sleet - crack

Sleigh ride - cocaine

Slick superspeed - methcathinone

Slime - heroin

Smack - heroin

Smears - LSD

Smoking - PCP

Smoke - heroin and crack; crack; marijuana

Smoke a bowl - marijuana

Smoke Canada - marijuana

Smoke-out - under the influence of drugs

Smoking gun - heroin and cocaine

Snap - amphetamine

Snappers - isobutyl nitrite

Sniff - to inhale cocaine; inhalant; methcathinone

Sniffer bags - $5 bag of heroin intended for inhalation

Snop - marijuana

Snort - to inhale cocaine; use inhalant

Snorts - PCP

Snot - residue produced from smoking amphetamine

Snot balls - rubber cement rolled into balls and burned

Snow - cocaine; heroin; amphetamine

Snowball - cocaine and heroin

Snow bird - cocaine

Snowcones - cocaine

Snow pallets - amphetamine

Snow seals - cocaine and amphetamine

Snow soke - crack

Snow white - cocaine

Soap dope - methamphetamine with a pinkish rose tint

Society high - cocaine

Soda - injectable cocaine used in Hispanic

communities

Softballs - depressant

Soles - hashish

Soma - PCP

Somali - methcathinone

Somatomax - GHB

Sopers - depressant

Spaceball - PCP used with crack

Space base - crack dipped in PCP; hollowed out cigar
refilled with PCP and crack

Space cadet - crack dipped in PCP

Space dust - crack dipped in PCP

Space ship - glass pipe used to smoke crack

Spark it up - to smoke marijuana

Sparkle plenty - amphetamine

Sparklers - amphetamine

Special "K" - ketamine

Special la coke - ketamine

Speed - methamphetamine; amphetamine; crack

Speedball - methylphenidate (ritalin) mixed with
heroin

Speedballs-nose style - the practice of snorting cocaine

Speed boat - marijuana, PCP, crack

Speed freak - habitual user of methamphetamine

Speed for lovers - MDMA

Speedball - heroin and cocaine; amphetamine

Spider blue - heroin

Spike - to inject a drug; needle

Spivias - amphetamines

Splash - amphetamine

Spliff - marijuana cigarette

Splim - marijuana

Split - half and half or to leave

Splivins - amphetamine

Spoon - 1/16 ounce of heroin;paraphernalia used to

prepare

heroin for injection

Spores - PCP

Sporting - to inhale cocaine

Spray - inhalant

Sprung - person just starting to use drugs

Square mackerel - marijuana, term from Florida

Square time Bob - crack

Squirrel - smoking cocaine, marijuana and PCP; LSD

Stack - marijuana

Stacking - taking steroids with a prescription

Star - methcathinone

Stardust - cocaine, PCP

Star-spangled powder - cocaine

Stash - place to hide drugs

Stash areas - drug storage and distribution areas

Stat - Methcathinone

Steerer - person who directs customers to spots for
buying crack

Stem - cylinder used to smoke crack

Stems - marijuana

Step on - dilute drugs

Stick - marijuana, PCP

Stink weed - marijuana

Stoned - under the influence of drugs

Stones - crack

Stoppers - depressant

Stove top - crystal methamphetamine

STP - PCP

Straw - marijuana cigarette

Strawberries - depressant

Strawberry - female who trades sex for crack or money
to buy crack; LSD

Strawberry fields - LSD

Strung out - heavily addicted to drugs

Stuff - heroin

Stumbler - depressant

Sugar - cocaine; LSD; heroin

Sugar block - crack

Sugar cubes - LSD

Sugar lumps - LSD

Sugar weed - marijuana

Sunshine - LSD

Super - PCP

Super acid - ketamine

Super C - ketamine

Super Grass - PCP

Super ice - smokable methamphetamine

Super joint - PCP

Super kools - PCP

Super weed - PCP

Supergrass - marijuana

Superman - LSD

Surfer - PCP

Sweet Jesus - heroin

Sweet Lucy - marijuana

Sweet stuff - heroin; cocaine

Sweets - amphetamine

Swell up - crack

Swishers - cigars in which tobacco is replaced with

marijuana

synthetic cocaine - PCP

Synthetic THT - PCP

top

T - cocaine; marijuana

T.N.T. - heroin; fentanyl

Tabs - LSD

Tail lights - LSD

Taima - marijuana

Taking a cruise - PCP

Takkouri - marijuana

Tango & Cash - fentanyl

Tar - opium; heroin

Tardust - cocaine

Taste - heroin; small sample of drugs

Taxing - price paid to enter a crackhouse; charging

more per vial depending on race of

customer or if not a regular customer

T-buzz - PCP

Tea - marijuana, PCP

Tea party - to smoke marijuana

Teardrops - dosage units of crack packaged in the

cut-off corners of plastic bags

Tecate - heroin

Tecatos - Hispanic heroin addicts

Teenage - 1/16 gram of methamphetamine

Teeth - cocaine; crack

Tension - crack

Tex-mex - marijuana

Texas pot - marijuana

Texas tea - marijuana

Thai sticks - bundles of marijuana soaked in hashish

oil; marijuana buds bound on short

sections of bamboo

THC - tetrahydrocannabinol

The beast - heroin

The C - methcathinone

The devil - crack

The witch - heroin

Therobolin - injectable steroid

Thing - heroin; cocaine; main drug interest at the moment

Thirst monsters - heavy crack smokers

Thirteen - marijuana

Thoroughbred - drug dealer who sells pure narcotics

Thrust - isobutyl nitrite

Thrusters - amphetamine

Thumb - marijuana

Tic - PCP in powder form

Tic tac - PCP

Ticket - LSD

Tie - to inject a drug

Tin - container for marijuana

Tish - PCP

Tissue - crack

Titch - PCP

Toilet water - inhalant

Toke - to inhale cocaine; to smoke marijuana

Toke up - to smoke marijuana

Toncho - octane booster which is inhaled

Tooles - depressant

Tools - equipment used for injecting drugs

Toot - cocaine; to inhale cocaine

Tooties - depressant

Tootsie roll - heroin

Top gun - crack

Topi - mescaline

Tops - peyote

Torch - marijuana

Torch cooking - smoking cocaine base by using a propane or

butane torch as a source of flame

Torch up - to smoke marijuana

Torpedo - crack and marijuana

Toss up - female who trades sex for crack or money to buy crack

Totally spent - MDMA hangover

Toucher - user of crack who wants affection before, during, or after smoking crack

Tout - person who introduces buyers to sellers

Toxy - opium

Toys - opium

TR-6s - amphetamine

Track - to inject a drug

Tracks - row of needle marks on a person

Tragic magic - crack dipped in PCP

Trails - LSD induced perception that moving objects

leave

multiple images or trails behind them

Trank - PCP

Tranq - depressant

Trap - hiding place for drugs

Trays - bunches of vials

Travel agent - LSD supplier

Trip - LSD; alpha-ethyltyptamine

Troop - crack

Trophobolene - injectable steroid

Truck drivers - amphetamine

TT1 - PCP

TT2 - PCP

TT3 - PCP

Tuie - depressant

Turbo - crack and marijuana

Turf - place where drugs are sold

Turkey - cocaine; amphetamine

Turnabout - amphetamine

Turned on - introduced to drugs; under the influence

Tutti-frutti - flavored cocaine developed by a Brazillian

gang

Tweak mission - on a mission to find crack

Tweaker - crack user looking for rocks on the floor

after a police raid

Tweaking - drug-induced paranoia; peaking on speed

Tweek - methamphetamine-like substance

Tweeker - methcathinone

Twenty - $20 rock of crack

Twenty-five - LSD

Twist - marijuana cigarette

Twists - small plastic bags of heroin secured with

a twist tie

Twistum - marijuana cigarette

Two for nine - two $5 vials or bags of crack for $9

2-for-1 sale - a marketing scheme designed to promote and

increase crack sales

Ultimate - crack

Uncle - Federal agents

Uncle Milty - depressant

Unkie - morphine

Up against the stem - addicted to smoking marijuana

Uppers - amphetamine

Uppies - amphetamine

Ups and downs - depressant

Utopiates - hallucinogens

Uzi - crack; crack pipe

top

V - the depressant Valium

Vega - a cigar wrapping refilled with marijuana

Viper's weed - marijuana

Vodka acid - LSD

Wac - PCP on marijuana

Wack - PCP

Wacky weed - marijuana

Wake ups - amphetamine

Wasted - under the influence of drugs; murdered

Water - methamphetamine, PCP

Wave - crack

Wedding bells - LSD

Wedge - LSD

Weed - marijuana, PCP

Weed tea - marijuana

Weightless - high on crack

West coast - methlylphenidate (ritalin)

West coast turnarounds - amphetamine

Wet - blunts mixed with marijuana and PCP

Whack - PCP and heroin

Wheat - marijuana

When-shee - opium

Whicked - heroin

Whippets - nitrous oxide

White - amphetamine

White ball - crack

White boy - heroin

White cloud - crack smoke

White cross - methamphetamine; amphetamine

White dust - LSD

White ghost - crack

White girl - cocaine; heroin

White-haired lady - marijuana

White horizon - PCP

White horse - cocaine

White junk - heroin

White lady - cocaine; heroin

White lightning - LSD

White mosquito - cocaine

White nurse - heroin

White Owsley's - LSD

White powder - cocaine; PCP

White stuff - heroin

White sugar - crack

White tornado - crack

Whiteout - isobutyl nitrite

Whites - amphetamine

Whiz bang - cocaine and heroin

Wild cat - methcathinone and cocaine

Window glass - LSD

Window pane - LSD

Wings - heroin; cocaine

Winstrol - oral steroid

Winstrol V - veterinary steroid

Witch - heroin; cocaine

Witch hazel - heroin

Wobble weed - PCP

Wolf - PCP

Wollie - rocks of crack rolled into a marijuana

cigarette

Wonder star - methcathinone

Woolah - a hollowed out cigar refilled with

marijuana and crack

Woolas - cigarette laced with cocaine; marijuana

cigarette sprinkled with crack

Woolies - marijuana amd crack or PCP

Wooly blunts - Marijuana and crack or PCP

Working - selling crack

Working half - crack rock weighing half gram or more

Works - equipment for injecting drugs

Worm - PCP

Wrecking crew - crack

X - marijuana; MDMA; amphetamine

X-ing - MDMA

XTC - MDMA

Yahoo/yeaho - crack

Yale - crack

Yeh - marijuana

Yellow - LSD; depressant

Yellow bam - methamphetamine

Yellow bullets - depressant

Yellow dimples - LSD

Yellow fever - PCP

Yellow jackets - depressant

Yellow submarine - marijuana

Yellow sunshine - LSD

Yen pop - marijuana

Yen Shee Suey - opium wine

Yen sleep - restless, drowsy state after LSD use

Yerba - marijuana

Yerba mala - PCP and marijuana

Yesca - marijuana

Yesco - marijuana

Yeyo - cocaine, Spanish term

Yimyom - crack

Ying Yang - LSD

Z - 1 ounce of heroin

Zacatecas purple - marijuana from Mexico

Zambi - marijuana

Zen - LSD

Zero - opium

Zig Zag man - LSD; marijuana; marijuana rolling papers

Zip - cocaine

Zol - marijuana cigarette

Zombie - PCP; heavy user of drugs

Zombie weed - PCP

Zooie - holds butt of marijuana cigarette

Zoom - PCP; marijuana laced with PCP

Zoomers - individuals who sell fake crack and then flee

If you found this book helpful please pick up my first book, Clean and Serene, for your child or someone you know struggling with addiction. Available online @ www.LloydHBell.com , Amazon and Barnes and Noble.

References

Addiction Glossary of Terms – Drug and AlcoholRelated Phrases – Defintions. (n.d.). Retrieved from http://www.projectknow.com/research/addiction-glossary-of-terms-and-phrases/

Drug terms. (n.d.). Retrieved from http://www.urban75.com/Drugs/drugterm.html

Doweiko, H. E. (2014). *Concepts of Chemical Dependency*. Pacific Grove,, CA: Cengage Learning.

Ruiz, P., Strain, E. C., & Langrod, J. (2007). *The substance abuse handbook*. Philadelphia: Wolters Kluwer Health/Lippincott Williams & Wilkins.

rolandwms (2017). *Cbt 2014*. [online] Slideshare.net. Available at: https://www.slideshare.net/rolandwms/cbt-2014 [Accessed 7 Jul. 2017]

www.ingramcontent.com/pod-product-compliance
Lightning Source LLC
Chambersburg PA
CBHW060919040426
42445CB00011B/691